D0015584

—— 7 DAYS OF ——
SIMPLICITY

TO

_____

FROM

_____

7 DAYS OF SIMPLICITY

A *Season of* *Living Lightly*

JEN HATMAKER

Abingdon Press

NASHVILLE

Jesus knew what He was talking about
when He told us to not store up too many treasures on this earth
but to live well and love well because, as it turns out,
that is what matters more than anything.

EVERY YEAR, I NEED A LITTLE LESS:

Less hustle, less busyness, less "success,"
less Big and More, less stuff.

AND I ALSO NEED A LITTLE MORE:

More family, more besties, more porches,
more dinners at home, more laughter,
more of our little church, more gratitude.

The longer I live, the more distilled it all gets: what matters,
what counts, what I love, where I want to be, and what I will
be glad I invested in forty years from now.

Sending love to every one of you finding deep delight in
exactly what you have and where you are, refusing the
More Monster and deciding that an old porch with your
beloveds is enough. Don't let anyone shame you out of
simplicity or contentment. I bet your life is spectacular
exactly how it is if you have eyes to see it.

CONTENTS

INTRODUCTION

THE SIMPLE LIFE, A NEW PERSPECTIVE

———

Have you ever been minding your own business, living your best life, until reality hip checks you into the wall and forces you to entertain a new perspective?

For years I didn't realize just how much abundance my family had or how blessed we were because so many others had more. When I wrote *7: An Experimental Mutiny Against Excess*, we were surrounded by extreme affluence, which tricks you into thinking you're in the middle of the pack.

I mean, sure, we have twenty-four hundred square feet to live in, but we haven't traveled to Italy, my kids are in public schools, and we don't even own a time-share with fully stocked shelves that contain no less than two bottles of Grey Poupon mustard at any given time. Who eats that stuff anyway?

It's easy to see yourself as somehow lacking or behind or lesser than when you constantly focus on the lives of others, specifically on what they do have that you don't have. But it gets uncomfortably fuzzy real quick once you spend time with people below your rung, people who see you as affluent, who wish they had half of what you do.

I was blissfully unaware that I reside in the top percentage of wealth in the world. (You probably do too: Make $35,000 a year? Top 4 percent. $50,000? Top 1 percent.) Our culture of excess and American-More has impaired our perspective; we are the richest people on Earth, praying to get richer. We're tangled in unmanageable debt while feeding the machine, because we both feel entitled to more and are terrified to fall behind our peers in a material-goods race that truly doesn't matter to begin with.

Our desire to fit in, to compete in the all-consuming consumer-goods game has done more than trash our budgets and our confidence, since we're continually comparing ourselves, our things, and our perceived happiness against the other 1-percenters. We're dragging our natural resources through the wringer without even realizing it.

Whether we're aware of it or not, the top percentage of consumers are affecting the quality of life for the rest of humanity due to unsustainable practices. Not convinced of our direct impact? According to the Ocean Conservancy, "Every year, 8 million metric tons of plastics enter our ocean . . . the equivalent of dumping one New York City garbage truck full of plastic into the ocean every minute of every day for an entire year!"[1] An easy way to lessen our burden on the earth is to say no to straws and single-use plastic bottles.

Okay, so we can totally start bringing our personal water bottle everywhere with us and actually allowing our precious lips to touch the glasses we drink from (or use metal, glass, or bamboo straws, if we must).

Awesome! We've saved the world!

Well, not so fast. There's still a LOT more we can do. We can be aware of not only what we use, but also where it goes when we're done with it. In 2012, the world's population produced 2.6 trillion pounds of garbage, the weight of about 7,000 Empire State Buildings (or, if you prefer another visual, it's enough to fill 822,000 Olympic-sized swimming pools[2]), and nearly half of that was organic trash, including the food we eat, the food animals eat, and horticultural waste.[3]

Sounds like a lot, right? But with numbers so large, with visual comparisons so seemingly impossible, it can be hard to feel any personal connection to it at all. This might help. According to a global risk consulting firm, the United States produces about 234 pounds of plastic waste per person per year.[4] That's a football player's worth of thrown-away plastic.

We need a new, open-eyed perspective. The personal responsibility to do our part in making healthier choices all around. And the urgency to do everything we can now, so that there's a better "later" for everyone, even after we're gone.

What does it communicate to our families, our communities, and our world when we consume and waste so much? Half the global population lives on less than $2 a day, and we can't manage a fulfilling life on twenty-five thousand times that amount? Or on fifty thousand times that amount?

When I realized just how rich we really are—and in many ways, how selfish and stubborn we can be—I started seeing my life, my belongings, my family, and my privilege with fresh eyes. It didn't take but a quick second to realize we had everything. I mean everything.

We've never missed a meal or even skimped on one. We have a beautiful home in a great neighborhood. Our kids are in a Texas exemplary school. We drive two cars under warranty. We've never gone a day without health insurance. Our closets are still overflowing. (Yes, even after the 7 experiment and all we have given away, we are not lacking in our clothing options, although we don't have as many items as we once had.) We still throw away uneaten food sometimes. And we still have to make a real effort to recycle what we can and be intentional about avoiding items that produce trash that will never disintegrate.

You'd better believe this realization knocked me on my butt for a bit until I accepted reality and made a game plan for moving forward with less and embracing the simplicity found in a more intentional pace of life. I needed to challenge my own beliefs about what it means to be content, to be successful, to be busy, to be a consumer, to be a follower, and to be rich.

BUT! Fear not—this shift in perspective came with new blessings too. I realized we didn't need all the things to be happy. In fact, having less and using less gave me a greater peace. It created new activities to participate in as a family, such as recycling, volunteering, and gardening. It meant we had more money each month to give to causes and organizations we support, and our eyes were opened to more needs and more opportunities where we could make a real difference in the lives of others.

Let's be honest—it also meant I had a little less laundry to do, a little less trash to take out, and a little less guilt after grocery shopping or clothes shopping.

Living with less GAVE US MORE. More time. More money. More joy. More healthy options. It allowed us to give others more too. And it sparked in me a renewed love for the earth, an awareness of our natural resources, and an excitement about the ways in which we can each do our part to ensure that we give our children and grandchildren a more beautiful planet.

God made us the caretakers of His creation. What an honor! How cool that we can grow our own food and flowers, take care of livestock, have less chaos and clutter in our homes, and support our local communities by making sustainable choices and purchases.

And it's so much fun to spend time outside! God made dirt and dirt don't hurt. Although it sometimes takes a few really good scrubbings to get it out from underneath your fingernails. But it's all good. Dirt is organic.

Anyway, *7 Days of Simplicity: A Season of Living Lightly* is a spiritual exercise both in living simply and in living more sustainably, taking care to develop an intentional practice of thankfulness and a less-is-more view of what we take and use of our natural resources.

Living simply is a path toward peace of mind and a peaceful home. Living sustainably is an act of grace and gratitude.

Oh! And one last note on the timeframe. As with the original 7, we're going to cover each of the same seven categories, but please feel free to do these at your own pace, according to whichever path is most reasonable for your life and family. Kind of like one of those Choose Your Own Adventure books you loved so much in elementary school.

Some may choose to focus on each of these seven areas over a week's time. There are always overachievers out there, and I'm jealous of you already.

Others might choose to dedicate a full month to each topic.

Some might take a more creative approach and choose any seven days within a month to dedicate to the themes.

No matter which approach you take, remember to step into this with grace, an open heart, and open eyes. There's no wrong answer. And there's no ultimate goal that everyone must aspire to achieve.

We can't all be perfect like Jesus or immaculately organized like Marie Kondo. I sure as heck don't have time for that. I'm doing well to make sure I brush my hair a few times a week. Thank the Lord for messy buns.

So, go forth and prosper. Play in the dirt. Clean out those old closets. Make time to do a whole lot of nothing. Eat good, healthy food. And breathe a little easier.

You've got this. And you're doing a great job already.

ONE

KITCHEN

*"So whether you eat or drink
or whatever you do, you should do it
all for God's glory."*

—1 CORINTHIANS 10:31

1

KITCHEN

THE BEAUTY OF
EATING SUSTAINABLY

We've all heard the phrase *sustainable living* by now, and it likely conjures ideas of tiny homes, fair-trade goods, off-grid compounds, solar panels, and the sweet older hippy woman at your local farmer's market who wraps all your purchases in newspaper, wears tie-dye like it's her religion, and has named all fifteen of her egg-laying chickens. *That's going to be me in thirty years, by the way. As long as I can still wear my cowboy boots.*

But what does eating sustainably mean? According to the Academy of Nutrition and Dietetics:

The concept of sustainability is applied toward the production of food or other plant or animal products using farming techniques and practices that help to conserve natural resources and have minimal impact on the environment. Sustainable agriculture enables us to produce healthful food without compromising future generations' ability to do the same. Sustainable eating is about choosing foods that are healthful to our environment and our bodies. [5]

Basically, the goal is to eat healthy while making the least amount of negative impact on the earth.

Sounds easy enough, right? But isn't this way of life just for granola people who have zero small children running around the house and who've made solar panels out of repurposed sunglasses?

Nope. Every single one of us has the ability to make small changes that lead to big results over time. As you'll see throughout the book, I'm not advocating for mindlessly discarding our possessions, for a complete life overhaul, or for unrealistic perspectives. My hope is that by being open-minded to the realities and opportunities around us, we can begin to live more lightly without losing any amount of joy.

Eating (and living) simply and sustainably really can be fun and incredibly rewarding when we look for ways to make it happen.

FAVORITES

Before you throw out all your canned goods and bags of snacks, remember this is a process, not a race. You don't have to GET RID OF anything. Nope. Not a thing. Not yet anyway and not unless you really want to.

As you begin this fun journey, simply start by being aware of what food items you already have and let that be your guide for how to use it and when to use it. And when it's time to buy more food, start by making choices that will provide you and your family with good, healthy food in minimal packaging (when possible). It's always great when you're able to make those purchases within your community too, whether at your local mom-and-pop grocery store, farmer's market, or Community Supported Agriculture (CSA) vendors.

Start small! Make one or two new choices when it comes to your food purchases and consumption and go from there. Whatever you do, know that *it is enough* because *you are enough*, and He is enough for all of our granola crunchiness.

As I reduce, He is enough.

As I simplify, He is enough.

He is our portion where food and clothes and comfort fall woefully short. He can heal us from greed and excess, materialism and pride, selfishness and envy. While our earthly treasures and creature comforts will fail us, Jesus is more than enough. You can believe that, sister.

In my privileged world where "need" and "want" have too often become indistinguishable, my only true requirement is the sweet presence of Jesus. And those fabric reusable grocery bags. If I could just remember to always put them back in the car after I've used them.

Drumroll please! Here are some kitchen-and-food-related favorites for some delicious 7-styled experiences:

- **FARMER'S MARKETS AND CSA VENDORS.** Have you looked into your local options? Farmer's markets are the equivalent of state fairs for food-loving adults, minus the questionable carnival rides. At my local markets (because there are several where I live, blessed be), there are always tables and tables of fresh seasonal fruits and vegetables, baked goods, CSA vendors with organic meats, honey, eggs, flowers, sometimes even clothing and jewelry and furniture. All I'm saying is, it's a solid hour or two of healthy entertainment, and you're sure to leave with some delicious food. Remember to bring your reusable bags!

- **REUSABLE AND RECYCLABLE PACKAGING.** Yes, I'm talking about those darn bags again. But there's more! I'm seeing more and more grocery stores selling bulk items and allowing the customer—that's you—to bring in your own storage containers. This works for beans, coffee, fruits and vegetables, and more. Sadly, it doesn't work for ice cream. Yet.

- **USE WHAT YOU HAVE BEFORE YOU BUY MORE.** Aha! Now we're cooking. Like I said, there's no reason for you to throw away any food items you already have unless they're expired or moldy. So get creative! Pull out an armful of your pantry items and see what kind of yummy concoctions you can make. Use those spices for once! Have an abundance of canned vegetables? Soup! Listen, leftover vegetable soup in a Tupperware container will stay fresh for months in your freezer. Ingredients for bread or brownies? Make them! There's zero shame in your game when you do the smart thing and use what you have before you rush out and buy more.

JEN'S TIPS AND TRICKS
FOR LIVING LIGHTLY

Because I am a weirdo, I love to bring my empty cardboard egg carton to the farmer's market, get my fresh dozen, and give the empty carton to my farmer for reuse. This makes me happy for weird reasons. Hey! Farmer's Markets are open in your communities tomorrow. Saturday is usually the day. You should go. **Buy squash.**

• **TRY A FAST.** Now, clearly I'm no doctor so please do consult with yours to make sure this is okay for you to do, but a fast doesn't have to be extreme. It can mean skipping a meal and drinking water and having a piece of fruit. *Raise your hand with me if you do that anyway.* It can mean choosing to skip meals during the day and waiting until you get home to have a hearty dinner. It can even mean focusing only on specific whole foods for a week. Fasting will give your digestive system a sweet little break and maybe even save you some money too.

REFLECTIONS ON
A SEASON OF SIMPLICITY

When I did the original 7 experiment, I had around 240 food items between my pantry, refrigerator, and freezer. I had two entire drawers of Tupperware containers and plastic sandwich bags because I sometimes forgot what I already had and kept buying more. Nearly everything in my pantry was processed, and that bothered me.

Occasionally I come across a book that is so insightful it is a real struggle not to plagiarize the entire thing. If I could insert the entire content of Michael Pollan's *In Defense of Food* right here, I would do it. It has revolutionized my ideas about food and nutrition.

But this is the main premise: Eat food. Not too much. Mostly plants.

What author Michael Pollan means by "food" is "real food" that came from the ground, a tree, a plant, or an animal without messing with it. Food that hasn't been loaded with corn syrup or injected with hormones. He writes not as a nutritionist overcomplicating something simple but on the authority of tradition and common sense.

Our grandmas ate local meat and vegetables from their gardens; we eat Pop Tarts and Velveeta. Today in America the culture of food is changing more than once a generation, which is historically unprecedented. This machine is driven by a $32 billion food-marketing engine that thrives on change for its own sake, not to mention constantly shifting nutritional science that keeps folding in on itself every few years.

One year, eggs are bad. The next year, eggs are good but carbs are bad. Soon they're going to say that water and air will kill you. And depending on where you live, that's unfortunately not too far off. *Looking at you, lawmakers and government in Detroit, Michigan.*

According to Michael Pollan, four of the top ten causes of death in America today are chronic diseases with well-established links to our industrialized diet: coronary heart disease, diabetes, stroke, and cancer. These health plagues remain rare in countries where people don't eat like us, even if their local diet is high in fat or carbs, the two dietary straw men America decided to fight. The basics of the Western diet include:

- The rise of highly processed foods and refined grains
- The use of chemicals to raise plants and animals in huge monocultures
- The abundance of cheap calories of sugar and fat
- The massive consumption of fast food
- The shrinking diversity of the human diet to a tiny handful of staple crops: notably wheat, corn,

and soy (thanks to vigorous lobbying and strategic subsidization by our government)

- The conspicuous absence of fruit, vegetables, and whole grains[6]

This bodes terribly for us, and it is downright disastrous for our children. In fact, US life expectancy was projected to rise indefinitely, but one data analysis from the *New England Journal of Medicine* suggests this trend is about to reverse itself due to the rapid rise in obesity, especially among children. Our kids are the first generation in the history of America that has a shorter life span than their parents.[7]

There is a way out of this madness, and we're part of the solution. After all, we get to vote three times a day with our forks and our wallets.

One thing I have recommitted to, now that I understand more today about global warming and climate change than I did then, is the contribution that the cattle industry makes to global warming. We consume the most meat, and we're also responsible for the largest amount of contributing factors to climate change.

I have renewed my commitment to eat far more meat-free meals, and I'm going to continue pushing back against the narrative that it won't matter, that one person making a difference in his or her life is silly. I'm going to resist and reject that notion, because I'd rather have a good answer

for my grandchildren and great-grandchildren when one day they ask me what I did to help our world. I am going to greatly increase how much less meat I eat, consume, and cook.

These days, I make more food from scratch than I ever did, and I'm being pretty careful about sourcing. I will say there's one thing I have thrown the towel in on permanently because I've had too many fails. I'm absolutely done with ever trying to make toffee or anything that requires cooking sugar.

Right this minute, I have a beautiful, perfectly seasoned cast iron skillet sitting on my porch where I burned sugar beyond oblivion. Mind you, it was the *third round* of sugar in an attempt to make homemade toffee, and I'm just done. Toffee, I realize that we are incompatible, and I am unable to conquer your sugary goodness when you are placed over heat, so I surrender. This is it. You win. I will buy my toffee when I have to have it, and I'm just going to make my peace with that.

FINAL THOUGHTS

"The naive believe anything,
but the prudent give thought to their steps."

—PROVERBS 14:15

Do you know what happened after eating only whole foods and virtually no fast food for a whole month? My pants were falling off. You're welcome for that visual.

But seriously, I felt energetic during my typical afternoon slump. My cheeks were rosy. My allergies disappeared. I didn't have any digestive issues. My canker sores went dormant. I swear, my eyes were whiter.

There's more. What used to take two hours shopping at the big store now only takes thirty-five minutes at the farmer's market. I've spent only half my grocery budget by not buying extra garbage. Plus, you can't imagine how much we've saved by eating mostly at home.

We're wasting less—you better believe new meals are created and leftovers get eaten—this was rare before 7, because we had so many other choices. (Why eat yesterday's food when you could have new food?) More than ever, the family has gathered around the kitchen, chopping and stirring and rehashing our day.

Maybe food simplification is a good idea for all of us and for more than one reason. Spiritual clarity and health come to mind. Waste reduction and time management and financial responsibility and gratefulness deserve some line space too. There are other things, but that's a decent start list.

Barbara Kingsolver is a better foodie (and writer) than me, so let's wrap up with her oh-so-good thoughts:

> *When my generation of women walked away from the kitchen we were escorted down that path by a profiteering industry that knew a tired, vulnerable marketing target when they saw it. "Hey, ladies," it said to us, "go ahead,*

get liberated. We'll take care of dinner." They threw open the door and we walked into a nutritional crisis and genuinely toxic food supply. . . . But a devil of a bargain it has turned out to be in terms of daily life. We gave up the aroma of warm bread rising, the measured pace of nurturing routines, the creative task of molding our families' tastes and zest for life; we received in exchange the minivan and the Lunchable.[8]

I'm certain there's a way back home. And I believe we can find it and nurture it, grow it and cook it, in ways that honor our bodies, our land, our families, and our God who gave us a whole earth full of delicious and nutritious choices.

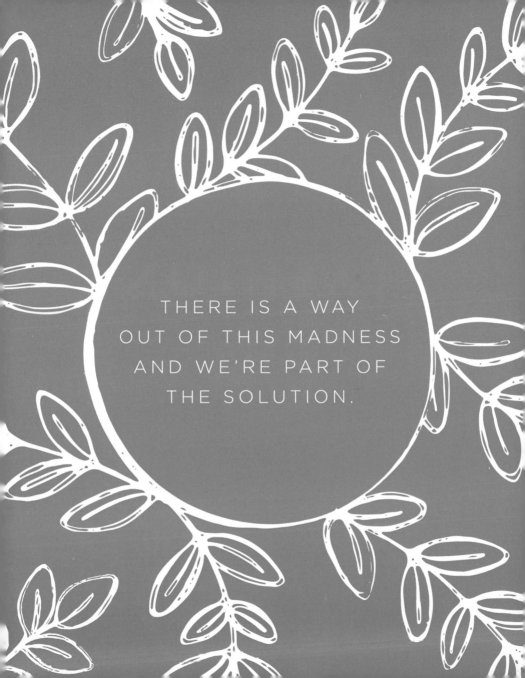

THERE IS A WAY
OUT OF THIS MADNESS
AND WE'RE PART OF
THE SOLUTION.

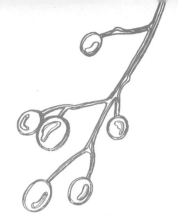

TWO

FASHION

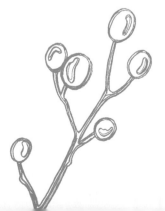

"Don't try to make yourselves beautiful on the outside, with stylish hair or by wearing gold jewelry or fine clothes. Instead, make yourselves beautiful on the inside, in your hearts, with the enduring quality of a gentle, peaceful spirit. This type of beauty is very precious in God's eyes."

—1 PETER 3:3-4

2

FASHION

WEARABLE WISDOM

As grown-up humans, one of the ways we express our unique style and personality is through our clothing choices. When we have endless options for clothing stores, designers, patterns, and colors—and a fair amount of disposable income—our closets can easily get crammed. Hence my shocking discovery of counting 327 items of clothing in my closet. Yes, that's just my stuff, not Brandon's or my kids' clothes. And I'm not even fashion-forward! What I'm saying is that if we aren't aware of what we have, what we actually need, and what we're buying, the stuff can pile up quickly without us even noticing until we're out of hangers or space.

But it wasn't always this way.

Back in the 1830s (yes, here's your history lesson for the week!), a decade before Elias Howe invented the sewing machine, people had far fewer clothing items. Most people had two outfits—one for everyday wear and one for Sunday worship—and maybe some people had another outfit for when the weather changed.[9] *Well*, you might think. *Naturally. They couldn't just make a quick trip to Target every time they stained a blouse.* And you'd be right.

Wealthy people could afford a few more items of clothing, and likely a personal seamstress, but still, they didn't have many clothes comparatively. Or closets, for that matter. Closets weren't a thing until the late 1870s when The Dakota apartment building in New York City used closets that were two-and-a-half feet deep and six feet wide—essentially a small, reach-in closet by today's standards—to appeal to wealthy tenants.[10] In case you were wondering how far we've come and how quickly we've gotten here, the walk-in closet appeared in the 1980s. And women's shoe collections were never the same.

My point in all of this is that while I'm guessing we really do need more than three outfits to wear throughout the course of a year, we probably don't need hundreds of items of clothing to make us legal to leave the house, while also showcasing our particular *je ne sais quoi*. You might only really need half of the clothing you own. *Gasp!* Too much change? Well, could you find five items of clothing that you don't really wear that you could donate? I bet you can.

I've had to work on this time and time again because even though I don't love shopping, believe it or not, it has become such a part of our culture. For some of us, it's more than a pastime; it's an escape from boredom, a form of procrastination, a way to connect with friends and family, and a form of giving gifts to those we love.

Trust me, nothing says, "I love you," like a pair of boxers with a big kissy face right on the butt.

No, I'm not suggesting you toss all your clothes and tear up your credit cards. What I'm saying is take some time to look through what you have. Everything. Yes, all the closets and dressers and storage boxes full of clothes. Just be aware of the items of clothing you currently own, then consider what you truly need. The next time you go shopping, keep that in mind. Do you *need* it? And when you have a few hours free and a hankering to tidy up or pare down, see what you can donate or give away that someone else might love and might really need.

FAVORITES

On any given day, I wear jeans and a T-shirt. My style is utterly unsophisticated; I look like a college girl who rolled out of bed five minutes before class—but who has

prematurely aged. In fact, I wear pretty much the exact same clothes to all my conferences. So, if you see pics posted, you may wonder *Is that the same conference?* No. I've just participated in five events in a row wearing the same outfit. Thou shalt not judge.

Anyhow, I'm a simple or possibly lazy dresser who doesn't spend much time thinking about my wardrobe.

Clothes are just not a huge deal to me. I mean, at least I'm not leaving my house in a bedsheet, right? *Now I wonder if I could make a look out of a flat sheet, a belt, and boots . . . hmm.*

Regardless of our style, the thing to remember is that all the clothing we own will one day leave our sweet little hands—it'll either be donated, repurposed, or recycled. Most of it will end up in the trash. In fact, since 85 percent of all textiles end up in the dump each year, that's the equivalent of one garbage truck full of clothes being burned or dumped in a landfill every second.[11] Every second. Can you believe it! Ugh, it makes my palms sweat to think about how many items I've bought over the years on a whim or because it was on sale or because I liked the color or pattern but didn't love it enough to keep it. Lesson learned!

Now that we are more educated shoppers, when it comes to simplifying the clothing itch, we have several options. Any of these are great, and if they spark a bit of creativity for you, even better!

- **BUY FEWER ITEMS.** Once we're aware of what we do have, we can be conscious consumers and picky shoppers. This can be hard for some when we see "SALE" signs, but do you really need that shirt in all thirteen colors? Take a deep breath and choose what you will really wear the most. Leave the rest for someone else to ooh and ahh over.

- **DONATE TO LOCAL ORGANIZATIONS.** This is a great practice to adopt on a yearly basis because the process of donating to others generally requires that you look through what you have first. This is also a smart way to see what you actually wear in a year. If you have had clothes in your closet for more than twelve months and they still have the tags on them, maybe someone else would wear it immediately and be ridiculously giddy to have scored such a sweet deal.

JEN'S TIPS AND TRICKS
FOR LIVING LIGHTLY

I just bribed Sydney to take Remy shopping in NYC without me in exchange for a small, discretionary budget. Am I the smartest person you ever met? Yes or no. I mean, I just avoided H&M in Times Square and am instead tucked into my dark, cozy hotel lobby by the fire with a mug of coffee. They are sending dressing room pics. All I do is win.

- **WEAR SUSTAINABLE FASHION.** Want to help the environment too? Organic clothing (organic cotton, silk, jute, wool, ramie, and bamboo) is produced with sustainable farming practices, which means the crops are grown without pesticides or other toxic chemicals.

- **UPCYCLE.** This is for you crafty ladies out there. One stubborn stain or rip in a piece of clothing doesn't mean it has to be thrown out. Get creative! Patches and cute appliques can cover most any stain. And have you seen the trends nowadays? Rips and holes in clothing are totally in! If you still don't like it, grab thread of any color and stitch it right up. Bonus points to those who add a fun twist and create leaves and patterns to their stitch work.

- **SHOP AT SECOND-HAND STORES.** One of my favorite options. If you need an item and it doesn't have to be brand-new (or you just need to get out of the house for some peace and quiet), your local second-hand store has untold treasures just waiting to be discovered! You can score some great deals at a fraction of the original price.

REFLECTIONS ON A SEASON OF SIMPLICITY

Unlike my sons who retire jeans with both knees blown out and the bottom hem shredded, most women cast off clothes we're just tired of or have outgrown. They're usually in great condition or could be reclaimed with one good dry cleaning. I know this because when I first began the 7 experiment, I had brand-new-looking clothes in my closet I hadn't worn for three years.

But what if, without spending a dime, we could freshen up our wardrobes and not feed the consumer machine more than it has already been fed? Clothes and accessories could be reincarnated into their second lives.

You could host your own Clothing Swap with friends and neighbors and coworkers. Bring snacks, chill the drinks, put on the music, and make a girls' night out of it. The more the merrier. Set up different stations: pants, purses, shoes, jewelry, shirts, accessories. Laugh and pretend you're kidding when you tell another woman if she touches that shirt, you'll cut her. Whatever isn't claimed can go to women's shelters and nonprofits.

It's the smallest idea, but it's a start. Maybe once we slow the cash hemorrhaging, some buried issues could surface, interrupting our default settings and raising questions we've never asked. And hey, at least someone would haul off the twenty items you've been waiting seven years to fit back into.

When I think back to 7, my biggest surprise was how easy it was to wear the same seven clothes for a month. I remember thinking that it just seemed so crazy of an idea, that this clothes thing was really going to be a challenge. So I was surprised by how wrong I was on that. It was a real relief not to be bogged down in all the clothes, the decisions, the washing, the fussing, the whatever, and also to realize that *nobody cares*. Part of my suspicion was that everyone was going to be like, *Why are you wearing the same clothes every day?* And nobody did that.

I thought this was probably going to be the hardest month for me and for my readers as well. When people first hear about the concept of 7, that month always stops people in their tracks for some reason. But my experience made me wonder if my readers had a similar surprise, and if it wasn't quite as hard as they thought.

The truth is, since I simplified my closet, I love that I have zero wardrobe planning every morning. I love the smaller pile of laundry in our basket. I love wearing jeans and a T-shirt every day. I love the simplicity and ease of it all. When I remember all of the clothes I purged, what I really see is wasted time and energy, more pointless work, self-obsession, the ironic "the more I have, the more I want" cycle. While my stuff is decreasing, what really matters (joy, peace, and a greater awareness of life) is increasing in equal measure.

Because I'm a reader and a lifelong learner, I slogged and underlined my way through *Consumed*, a remarkable book on the shifting nature of capitalism. After reading most paragraphs twice, the facts settled nicely in the brain space between the "Common Sense" and "Don't Be an Idiot" sections.

I learned that marketing used to represent basic needs of humans, without much embellishment or hyperbole. Certainly, the Third World still has these needs in spades—to the detriment of life and health and family—but no consumer power. Thus, Big Marketing turned to the wallet of the privileged, invented a bunch of fake needs (prepackaged sugar water, collagen moisturizer, Tide to Go pens, the Slanket), and disregarded the people who were actually dying every day from a lack of basics, exposed to the seductions of the consumer marketplace but without the means to participate in it.

In this new epoch in which the needy are without income and the wealthy are without needs, radical inequality is simply assumed . . . Inequality leaves capitalism with a dilemma: the overproducing capitalist market must either grow or expire. If the poor cannot be enriched enough to become consumers, then grown-ups in the First World who are currently responsible for 60 percent of the world's consumption, and with vast disposable income but few needs, will have to be enticed into shopping.[12]

Well, crap. This is why we have too many items in our closets, our homes, our lives. I am a part of the problem, a contributing member of inequality. Every time I buy another shirt I don't need or a seventh pair of shoes for my daughter, I redirect my powerful dollar to the pockets of consumerism, fueling my own greed and widening the gap. Why? Because I like it. Because those are cute. Because I want that.

These thoughts burden me holistically, but the trouble is, I can rationalize them individually. This one pair of shoes? Big deal. This little outfit? It was on sale. This micro-justification easily translates to nearly every purchase I've made. Alone, each item is reduced to an easy explanation, a harmless transaction.

But what if all my silly little individual purchases *do* matter? What if I joined a different movement, one that was less enticed by luxuries and more interested in justice? What if I believed that every dollar spent was vital, a potential soldier in the war on inequality?

When choices overwhelm me, Jesus makes it simple again: "Love your neighbor as yourself." We cannot carry the gospel to the poor and lowly while emulating the practices of the rich and powerful. Let's align ourselves correctly, sharing in the humble ministry of Jesus, knowing one day we'll feast at His table in splendor. I'll be wearing my favorite old yoga pants.

FINAL THOUGHTS

"The Levite asked ...
'If I stop to help this man, what will happen to me?'
The good Samaritan (responded):
'If I do not stop to help this man, what will happen to him?'"
—MARTIN LUTHER KING JR.

I've come a long way from my crowded-closet days at the beginning of the original 7 experiment. Do I still have more than I need? Yes. Do I try to be aware of what I buy? Also yes. We're not striving for perfection here. We're making progress.

Plus, I have to admit, there's a beauty in owning fewer things. And not just because it's easier on my wallet. It's because it makes it a lot easier to choose an outfit if I have a few tried-and-true pieces I love, and I don't have to sift through racks of clothes I hardly ever wear.

In terms of consignment and thrift shopping, I have learned the most from my daughter Sydney since the original writing. She was in elementary school then but she is a sophomore in college now and she and her friends are outstanding at this. They buy almost exclusively thrift and when they buy new, they're really careful about which vendor they buy from. They follow the source all the way to the beginning of the supply chain and are really careful with how they spend their money.

One thing she has taught me is about all these amazing online consignment sites (that didn't exist at the time of the original book) like Poshmark that provide access to gently used clothes and accessories and shoes from other consumers all around the United States. If you were once locked into whatever could be found in your local thrift store, now people are swapping and buying from one another all around the country and not contributing to additional waste in terms of manufacturing new products, expensive shipment options, and questionable supply chains.

What we still end up getting is new-to-us products that we love, that we've picked out, that are in our wheelhouse, without dumping more money into the bottomless pit of clothes, shoes, and accessories. It's a really good way to pull out of the system and not sacrifice fashion as you're refreshing your wardrobe.

Want a pro tip? Play dress-up! To see what you really do have, play around in your closet, experiment, and put together fifteen to twenty smart outfits you really like. Take pictures of them, including shoes and accessories, and create a folder on your phone. That way, if you're in a rush or a rut, you can flip through your pictures and pick out an outfit you've already preapproved. If you do this long enough, you might even begin to see that you can, in fact, get by with fewer items of clothing. And less stress, for heaven's sake.

The next generation is doing a great job of this. They take a lot of flak for being lazy or entitled, but that is not my experience with them. My experience is that they are savvy consumers, that they are paying attention approximately a hundred times more than I was at their age. They are responsible voters who vote with their dollars, and I feel very hopeful about the next generation.

In my mind, being a good Samaritan and helping our neighbors in need also means being good stewards of what we have. And I'm all about doing the best we can with what we have.

So take a week, a month, or a handful of days to meditate on this topic and take stock of the clothing you own. Marie Kondo's advice is to hold up an item and ask yourself if it sparks joy in you. We can take it a step further! When you're looking through your items, ask yourself if each one helps you simplify your life in some way.

While that little black sequined party dress might spark joy in my heart, my head knows I'm never going to be able to fit my body in it again. Does it simplify my life to keep staring at it every year when I have my closet purge? No. Time to let it go.

BEING A
GOOD SAMARITAN
AND HELPING OUR
NEIGHBORS IN NEED
ALSO MEANS BEING
GOOD STEWARDS
OF WHAT WE
HAVE.

THREE

STUFF

"Stop collecting treasures for your own benefit on earth, where moth and rust eat them and where thieves break in and steal them. Instead, collect treasures for yourselves in heaven, where moth and rust don't eat them and where thieves don't break in and steal them. Where your treasure is, there your heart will be also."

—MATTHEW 6:19-21

3

STUFF

MORE THAN ENOUGH

—

About three times a year, I feel The Purge coming on. I rant around the house, screaming at our stuff: "What is all this? How did this get here? Why do we have so much junk? How am I supposed to keep up with all this? Where did this all come from?" And then I remember, *I bought it all.*

Oops.

Now, it's true that some stuff is simply the inevitable outcome for a family of seven—after all, we can't all run around Austin, Texas, wearing fig leaves and flipflops. But we don't need so much that it fills every closet, every drawer, and shelf. There's something to be said for a clean, decluttered closet. A tidy shelf. A child's bedroom that does not have fifteen socks, three cups, a broken toy, and a ballcap thrown under the bed as if that was the easiest way to clean the room. I mean, it works, *technically*, but there's a better way.

The first step was to acknowledge how it all got there: I bought it. (Unless Brandon bought it. In that case, he can defend himself.)

The second step was to acknowledge why: because I wanted it. Or the kids wanted it. Or it was on sale. Or . . . pick a reason.

I also had to admit that I am a schizophrenic consumer.

When I first did The Purge back in 2010, I gave away 202 items from just my closet. Eek! When it came to the rest of the house, the trend continued. I had some cool stuff, but it was truly more than I needed. For example, I had about a hundred books on God. I had another sixty on women's issues. This didn't include my fiction, memoirs, essays, global issues, cookbooks, biographies, and reference books. Oh okay, and commentaries, mysteries, poetry anthologies, parenting books, and autobiographies. And history books. And maps and atlases. And humor essays. Books on tape.

I also had lots of movies. Like four drawers full of VHS tapes and no VHS player.

And about three-hundred-jillion blankets. Because.

I can honestly say that until I actually pulled out everything I owned and counted up what I had, I was woefully ignorant, not only about the money we spent to have a house full of things but also that we had so many *things* that we could have already given to people who really needed them.

So you know what we did? We got together with some of our dearest friends who were also excited about getting rid of stuff, and together, we liquidated tons of items—

beds, linens, microwaves, couches, TVs, tables and chairs, dishes, pictures, and clothing. In fact, we were able to fully furnish an apartment for a family of Burmese refugees who only had the clothes they were wearing when they landed in Texas. That family still had huge obstacles to overcome—financial independence, language acquisition, education, empowerment, community—an overwhelming transition in an unfamiliar country. But that first night in Texas, they slept on their own sheets in their own beds at their own apartment.

Because we had more than enough, God was able to orchestrate a new beginning for a beloved family who had known far too much violence and fear. Thanks to the efforts of many, they experienced safety and love, deep in the heart of Texas.

FAVORITES

Okay, now before you get your hackles up, no . . . I'm not making you get rid of anything. You don't have to do The Purge. You don't have to give away a carload of your most favorite possessions to your local thrift store. You don't have to toss out all of your books and DVDs and throw blankets and collectible figurines, *sohelpyouGod*.

So chillax.

All I request of you again, dear reader, is that you make yourself fully and graciously aware of what you have. That's it! Once you see what you have, you're in a much better place to make decisions on what else you do or don't need, how you might fare just fine with fewer things, and how you could possibly find new homes for items you no longer use or want.

Taking these small steps will no doubt help your budget while also reducing your carbon footprint. You may have heard that term before but aren't sure what it actually means. According to Nature.org, "A carbon footprint is the total amount of greenhouse gases (including carbon dioxide and methane) that are generated by our actions."[13] This includes what we buy, what we eat, what we wear, and even what we choose to watch as entertainment. Americans have one of the highest rates in the world—no surprise there—and that also means we have one of the most compelling reasons to do our part to simplify our lives all around so that we can be healthier and help make the world healthier too.

For those of you who prefer to take an easy, meandering approach to simplification, you can start by going room to room and taking mental notes. I'm going to guess that once you see what you have, you might start to get some ideas of what you can likely live without.

For you adventurers, if you're in the mood to go spelunking in your closets or your basement or attic space this week, leave no box or bin unopened. Leave no shelf undiscovered. (And leave no children behind if they accompany you into the dark recesses of your dwelling space. They'll be hungry in a few hours.)

So how to begin?

Well, we've already talked about food and clothes, so those two get a pass for now. What we'll focus on today is the majority of our possessions, otherwise known as *stuff*. Here are some tips to get your stuff under control:

- **SELL YOUR STUFF AT SPECIALTY STORES.** When it comes to entertainment items (books, music, movies, etc.), there are specialty stores that will give you cash for these items! Research your area to see if local stores are buying used books, music, and other types of media. If you strike out there, try your local library or community centers to see if they have a need for these items. Same goes for furniture. Contact your local consignment stores to see if they can sell your old dinette set, the antique clock your dog runs from

every time it chimes, or your vintage dish set from 1962. Might as well see if you can make a little money for releasing these things.

- **WHERE DOES IT BELONG?** This quick organizational tip will save you time and energy from not having to walk all over the house: Put all your similar items together in one space. Have a ton of family sports equipment or hobby supplies? Store it all together in a closet, garage, or designated workspace. Have a literal bucketful of pens and pencils scattered all over the house? Put them where you actually need them—in an office drawer. In a pencil holder in the kitchen or on bedroom desks. The same can be said for scissors. I have four pairs of kitchen scissors simply because I never could find them and kept buying more. Store your similar-use items together where they make sense so you can find them easier.

- **HOST A GROUP SWAP MEET.** Do you have a good amount of items your friends and neighbors might need or want? While you could absolutely have a yard sale, why not create a money-free meeting where everyone brings twenty or thirty items to swap? The rules here are simple: take what you actually want or need and leave the rest to be donated to a local charity. This way, you don't spend any money, and you hopefully bring home fewer items than you left with. This is a fun way to meet your neighbors and see your friends. Who knows, you might discover someone near you who has deeper needs (food, funds, transportation) you could help with, or you could reach out to community groups on their behalf.

- **STORE IT BUT DON'T IGNORE IT.** There are things we own that we don't really need but we can't bear to part with them for sentimental reasons. Your baby's first outfit. That ticket stub from the first date with your spouse. Pictures from spring break and graduation. Fear not! You don't have to ditch these wonderful memories. Instead, store them responsibly (in plastic bins in temperature-controlled conditions) and look through them now and then. As much as I'd love to advocate for cardboard storage boxes, they invite all manner of bugs, so choose plastic storage containers with a tight-sealed lid. And think ahead as to where they should be stored in your home. Old pictures are fun to look at, but if you keep them in a hot attic space, they may melt or fade, so choose a closet shelf instead on the main floor. Or better yet—digitize all of your family pictures and videos so everyone can enjoy them electronically.

JEN'S TIPS AND TRICKS
FOR LIVING LIGHTLY

There is almost NOTHING that doesn't have the capacity to get better, to change, to spark into newness. I always justify the rut by imagining that an entire overhaul is too hard, but the truth is, it is usually just a few nudges, some small changes, a turn of a rusty dial or two and just like that, the thing is in motion.

REFLECTIONS ON
A SEASON OF SIMPLICITY

When I first began the 7 experiment all those years ago, I lived in a home with 2,465 square feet, four bedrooms, two living rooms, two and a half bathrooms, nine closets, twenty-six cabinets, three bookshelves, and ten dressers and armoires. Every last one of these spaces was packed full. Now, as much as I'd love to blame Target and Amazon for putting all of this stuff in my house, I'm the one who bought these goods, so I can't really shift blame that much.

What I can do, however, is open my eyes to the reality of drive-by consumerism—those commercials, jingles, ads, newspapers, magazines, and more. Thousands of companies are fighting every day for my attention and my money, and I'm sad to say I've fallen for their schemes more times than I could ever count.

I see it (on you, on them, in their house, at Target, on TV). Within a millisecond, I manufacture a need for it. Then I buy it. I use it a little or not at all. Then I store it, shelve it, stack it, stuff it, or get tired of it, then wage war against it one day when all my little things are strewn about as escapees from their shelves and drawers.

I could blame Big Marketing for selling me imagined needs. I could point a finger at culture for peer pressuring me into having *nicer things* or the newest gadget that will surely save me time and money as soon as I hand over my credit card. I might implicate modern parenting, which encourages endless purchases for the kids, ensuring they aren't the "have-nots" in a sea of "haves." I could just dismiss it all with a shrug and casual wave of the hand, *Oh, you know me! Retail therapy!*

But if I'm being truthful, this is a sickening cycle of consumerism that I perpetuate constantly. I used to pardon excess from the tension of the gospel by saying, "Oh, it doesn't matter how much you have; it's what you do with it." But that exemption is folding in on itself lately. Plus, let's be honest: What does "it's what you do with it" even mean? Are we really doing something honorable with our stuff other than consuming it? I'm not sure carting it all off after we're bored with it is a helpful response, since we just replace it with more.

But I have a better idea—what if we stopped participating, stopped listening and watching and lusting after all of these commercials that subtly tell us we're not good enough as we are with what we already have? What if we were content with what we have and who we are?

It's a not-so-revolutionary idea that has the potential to revolutionize our homes, our self-esteem, and our wallets.

Still on the fence about a purchase? Sometimes we need a grandmother's wisdom. Some of the greatest advice I've heard around emotional purchases was when someone's grandmother told them if they really wanted something to wait a month. By the end of the month you've likely forgotten all about the thing. In that case, problem solved. If, a month later, you decide you really do need or want the item, go get it.

FINAL THOUGHTS

*"When I was a child, I used to speak like a child, reason like a
child, think like a child. But now that I have become
a man, I've put an end to childish things. Now we see a reflec-
tion in a mirror; then we will see face-to-face.
Now I know partially, but then I will know completely in the
same way that I have been completely known."*

—1 CORINTHIANS 13:11–12

A child says, "me." An adult says, "us." Maturity
deciphers need from want, wisdom from foolishness.
Growing up means curbing appetites, shifting from "me"
to "we," understanding that private choices have social
consequences and public outcomes.

So now that we are aware, enlightened if you will, let's
be consumers who silence the screaming voice that yells,
"I WANT!" and instead listens to the quiet "we need,"

the marginalized voice of our friends and family and neighbors and the worldwide community we belong to.

We top the global food chain through no fault or credit of our own. I've asked God a billion times why I still have so much while others have so little. Why do my kids get full bellies? Why does water flow freely from my faucets? Why do we get to go to the doctor when we're sick? There is no easy answer. The *why* definitely matters, but so does the what.

What do we do with our riches? What do we do with our privileges? What should we keep? What should we share? My thought is that I'd better address this inequality since Jesus clearly identified the poor as His brothers and sisters—and my neighbor.

What if we tried together? What if a bunch of Christians wrote a new story, becoming the conscious and educated consumers the earth is groaning for? I suspect we'd find that elusive contentment, storing up treasures in heaven like Jesus told us to. I'm betting our stuff would lose its grip, and we'd discover riches contained in a simpler life, a communal responsibility. Perhaps the secret to happiness is right under our noses. Maybe we don't recognize satisfaction because it is disguised as radical generosity, a strange misnomer in a consumer culture.

Richard Rohr described American Christians in *Simplicity*:

> *We're just about to become adults, to honestly let the Gospel speak to us, to listen to what Jesus says, in no uncertain terms, about poverty and about leading a simple life in this world, a life that shows trust in God and not*

in our own power and weapons. God never promised us security in this world. God promised us only truth and freedom in our hearts. What does all this mean for us? It means that we're on the way.[14]

Let's be well on our way to becoming responsible adults and listening, open-hearted humans. Educated and intentional consumers. Compassionate givers. Reverent takers. Together, we can prove this theory correct.

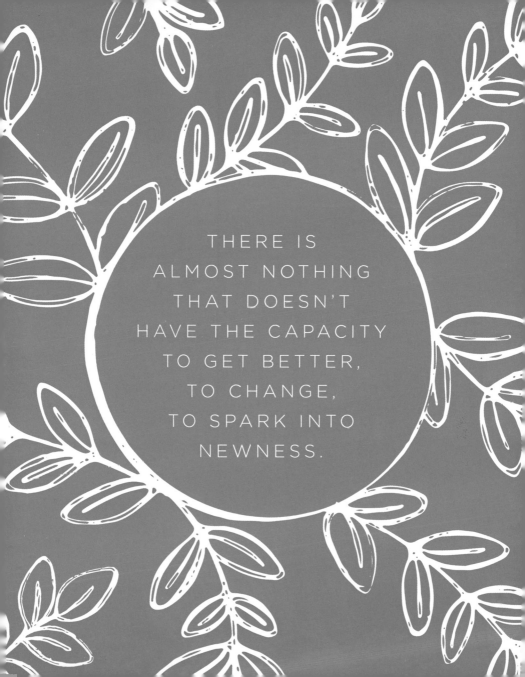

THERE IS
ALMOST NOTHING
THAT DOESN'T
HAVE THE CAPACITY
TO GET BETTER,
TO CHANGE,
TO SPARK INTO
NEWNESS.

FOUR

STREAMING

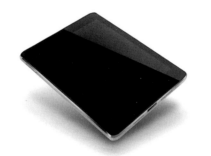

"He has told you, human one, what is good and what the Lord requires from you: to do justice, embrace faithful love, and walk humbly with your God."

—MICAH 6:8

4

STREAMING

DROWNING OUT THE NOISE

Think about all of the technology in the average American house. There's likely a TV (or three), computers, smart phones, tablets, a radio, maybe even an e-reader, a smart watch, Bluetooth noise-cancelling headphones, and video game consoles. I mean, in our house alone we have four gaming systems, two MacBooks and one desktop computer, five TVs, tons of cell phones (two of the "i" variety), a DVR, two DVD players, three handheld Nintendo DSs, and three stereos.

We have hundreds of choices on television programming, an infinite number of websites to browse, and music subscription services so we're never without our favorite songs. We even have white noise machines so we can listen to something while we pretend we're not listening to anything.

It's stunning, since I didn't have a computer, an email address, or cable until 2005. And like most families, we went from zero to full-blown addiction in just a few years. I don't know how we even lived before Al Gore invented the internet.

Sure, all of these electronic gadgets are fine and dandy, but what gives? When's the last time you sat in silence and read a book, prayed, thought about your goals and dreams, or God forbid . . . did . . . nothing? Are we really that afraid of our own thoughts or having real conversations with people that we fill our eyes and ears and brains with so much external noise that we devolve into drooling, plugged-in zombies?

I mean, have you seen (or smelled) a room full of teenagers lately? This is entirely possible.

But I don't think we have to tolerate the status quo simply because that's how most people live these days. In fact, I think it's our duty to break free from the confines of technology now and then so we can remember what it is like to be free. Free from the constant nag of email and social media apps. Free from hostile news programs and violent shows. Free from yelling and anger and frustration and predictions of a bleak future if we don't jump on the bandwagon right this minute.

We have the power and the sense to push pause any time we want to. And I say we start doing it on the regular. We can drown out the constant hum. We can unplug and not

only survive but thrive! We can take our time back and, in doing so, take control over our daily schedule and maybe even gain a little more sanity and simplicity in the process.

FAVORITES

Is it really groundbreaking news that too much media is bad for us? Is anyone thinking, *You know what my kids need? More screen time.* Far too often I see couples having dinner in silence, checking their phones, as if email or news or a text cannot wait one hour. Entire families are at the restaurant looking down into their handheld gadgets instead of eating or, heaven forbid, talking to each other. And if they do this in public, you know as soon as they get home they spread out all over the house, separating themselves even more to be alone with whatever is on their little screen or to avoid real face-to-face conversations with family members.

Isn't that sad? We're missing out on so much that we can never get back. Cramming our skulls full of a million unimportant voices and ignoring interactions with family and friends—not to mention avoiding our own thoughts and internal nudges. All because of a need to feel like we're connected, when what we're really doing is *disconnecting a little each day.*

Lots of experts are weighing in on this. It turns out, all this input isn't just annoying; it's troubling. A *New York Times* article, citing dozens of sources, reported that this is your brain on computers:

> *Scientists say juggling e-mail, phone calls and other incoming information can change how people think and behave. They say our ability to focus is being undermined by bursts of information.*
>
> *These play to a primitive impulse to respond to immediate opportunities and threats. The stimulation provokes excitement—a dopamine squirt—that researchers say can be*

addictive. In its absence, people feel bored. The resulting distractions can have deadly consequences, as when cell-phone-wielding drivers and train engineers cause wrecks. And for millions of people these urges can inflict nicks and cuts on creativity and deep thought, interrupting work and family life.[15]

Even after this rapid-fire multitasking ends or we're able to separate ourselves from technology for longer periods of time, fractured thinking persists because evidently our brains have adapted to shorter attention spans and the need to always be busy or distracted. Not convinced? A 2018 Nielsen study might make your head spin right off your pretty little neck:

US adults are spending more than 11 hours a day on average—or about two-thirds of their waking time—consuming media in some form . . . TV, radio, and digital households and consumers, activities like watching TV and DVDs, listening to the radio, visiting apps on a smartphone or tablet, and using the internet and game consoles.[16]

I am completely guilty of this, and it gives me ping-pong brain. It is increasingly hard to focus on one task for longer than twenty minutes without succumbing to an alternate source.

But that's not the worst of it. A new study surveyed over 1,000 American workers and found that people on average spend more than five hours per day checking their email.[17] FIVE. HOURS. If that doesn't make your head spin, I don't know what will.

So the big question is—what do we do about it? How do we take our time back without quitting our jobs, becoming oblivious to everything going on in the world around us, and cutting communication with friends and family unless they're cool with note-carrying pigeons? Can we manage a simpler approach to communication and the consumption of media without losing our sanity?

Why, yes! Glad you asked. Here are some suggestions to help you reclaim your time, reconnect with your tribe, and calm the busy buzzing in your brain.

- **DESIGNATE ONE NIGHT A WEEK AS BEING TECH-FREE AND READ A BOOK OR WORK ON YOUR HOBBY INSTEAD.** (No, you do not get a free pass if your hobby is tech-related. Yes, you can DVR your favorite show if you must.) If you make it past the first week, see if you can go the whole month being tech-free for one night a week.

- **TURN YOUR TEXT NOTIFICATIONS OFF AT BEDTIME.** This one's tough, but you can do it. You won't get the sleep you need if you're constantly being awakened by notification lights and noises. Want to take it a step farther? Leave your phone in the kitchen when you go to bed so it's not within arm's reach.

- **TRY CHECKING YOUR EMAIL AND SOCIAL MEDIA PAGES ONLY AT A FEW SPECIFIC TIMES EACH DAY.** Current research says you should try to check email no more than three times each day. That might take some self-control to not open a new computer screen or grab the phone every five minutes, but you can leave the phone in another room so it's not next to you. And computer apps like SelfControl and others can help by blocking certain websites within the hours you designate so you can focus on work and avoid distractions.

- **LEAVE YOUR PHONE AT HOME AND GO FOR A WALK OR SPEND A FEW HOURS OUTSIDE.** No, you won't get jumped by a bear. And chances are, a UFO won't land in front of you, so you don't need a camera either. You'll be just fine.

- **HAVE KIDS? START A WEEKLY GAME NIGHT AND PUT ALL ELECTRONICS AWAY FOR A FEW HOURS.** You might have to package this in a creative way at first, but I'm guessing your kids will love being able to spend time with you, especially if there's a fun game involved.

JEN'S TIPS AND TRICKS FOR LIVING LIGHTLY

So here is me suggesting to you that if the people you follow regularly make you feel bad, sad, mad, or less, unfollow, mute, or hide them and see if you don't notice an immediate difference.

- **HAVE A ROOMMATE OR A FAMILY OR A NEIGHBOR?** Strike up a real conversation and ask about their day and their life. You might learn something new and exciting, such as when the next neighborhood potluck is being held. Never miss an opportunity to eat mashed potatoes with perfectly good strangers.

REFLECTIONS ON
A SEASON OF SIMPLICITY

Do you remember when we used to mail letters and read the paper and leave messages on answering machines? We were not available every second, and my gosh, I miss that. It seems I cannot be unplugged for three hours without someone asking, "Where are you? I've e-mailed you and sent you three texts." My time no longer belongs to me, and if I disconnect for a few hours, people take it as a personal affront. I'm guessing it happens to you too.

But is that my problem or theirs?

Hmm.

Take something away, and your habits become clear. Parts of my day I don't miss media at all because I'm working or running errands or meeting with people. But I can easily identify the sections of my daily routine

7 DAYS OF SIMPLICITY

when media is a habit, a faithful companion to that time slot or task:

- Morning coffee + *The Today Show*
- Prewriting procrastination = Facebook and obsessive sing-alongs to the *Hamilton* soundtrack
- Folding laundry + *The Mindy Project*
- Mental writing break = cooking blogs and www.failblog.org
- Lunch at the table + Food Network
- Post-kid bedtime = Binge-watching everything

Once we realized just how much media we consume in any given week, Brandon and I made some changes (like having a weekly family game night and reducing the amount of TV we watch before bed), and let me tell you—the resulting periods of family face time and blessed silence have been awesome.

Our house even feels peaceful—well, as peaceful as a house with five kids and all their homies can feel. I *like* the missing white noise of media. I *like* the silence during the day. I *like* the alternative rhythms we're discovering. Like:

- Cooking together

- Walks after dinner

- Porch time with our friends

- Sydney's endless craft projects at the table

- Dinner with neighbors

- Actual phone calls and not just endless texting

- Finally making a dent in reading all those books I own, one by one

- Caleb's obsession with fishing

These discoveries are emerging out of the black hole of media. It's not rocket science; there's just space for them now. With the TV off, we ask, "What else can we do?" With the Wii packed away, the kids invent their own games. With an hour to kill after dinner, we grab Lady and hit the sidewalk. Some of this is out of boredom, some out of desperation, but still. We are making intentional changes to bring more peace and simplicity into our lives. And I love it!

Several times, as I realized I was caught up on correspondence, done with laundry, and finished with my to-do list, God whispered: "Hi there."

My communion with God suffers not for lack of desire but time. And let's be honest: I say I don't have time, yet I found thirty-five minutes for Facebook and an hour for my shows. I found fifteen minutes for the radio and twenty-four minutes for a missed TV episode. So when I say I don't have time, I'm a gigantic liar.

I have time. I just spend it elsewhere.

Without the noise and static, I'm learning about that

walk humbly part. It's in the silence that God trains me for acting justly and loving mercy. Being aware of God's presence is a powerful catalyst for courage and change.

FINAL THOUGHTS

"Don't be anxious about anything; rather, bring up all of your requests to God in your prayers and petitions, along with giving thanks. Then the peace of God that exceeds all understanding will keep your hearts and minds safe in Christ Jesus."

—PHILIPPIANS 4:6-7

The hardest area for light living for me (which I am sad to say has not gotten better but probably worse since the original book) is technology. Since the time 7 was written in 2010, the sheer number of additional apps and platforms and social media outlets and opportunities to look at my phone for literally every need anywhere,

anytime feels like it has quadrupled. I wish that I could report that reform had real staying power, but it continues to be probably our most challenging area of excess. And it's the same for our kids.

When I originally wrote 7, I had only three kids and they were in elementary school and early middle school. Now I've got teenagers and young adults. My oldest son is 21. Their media and technology life and consumption has also increased. I don't have a simple solution out of this. And in so many ways, media and technology have improved our lives and improved the world.

So, I don't think this is a simple matter of saying we

should just throw all technology out. But I do believe the need to address this area is more important than ever, and I do believe it is possible to put restraints on media and technology consumption, even now. It's going to take our own decisiveness and creativity to figure out how to use our senses to experience the world and people right where we are, not always looking at a screen, so we can continue experiencing the world like every generation has done before ours.

I know in the big scheme of things, a media fast is not headlining news. Game night is not breaking any attendance records. And no one is going to give me a pat on the back for finally finishing another book. But I gotta tell you, it's given me a much-needed perspective on what really matters and what doesn't.

One tip that works for me, in terms of spending less time in front of a screen, is that I never keep my phone in my bedroom. At night I charge my phone in the living room, and I never bring it into the bedroom. It is not the last thing I see nor the first thing I see in the morning. This is a very small victory admittedly, but it helps. It means I'm having human interaction at the end and beginning of every day as I spend time with my family.

We also turn off our kids' data at a certain time at night, which they hate. There's been an absolute mutiny over that in our house. But Brandon and I decided we still have to be the grown-ups in the room, even though it seems like nobody else on earth has any restraint at all, especially when it comes to kids and media and technology consumption.

Since the original writing we've learned what screen time does to our children's brains while they're forming. Their brains are still creating so many pathways and are different than our fully formed adult brains. The data is still young, but we do know the overload of screen time is interrupting their sleep patterns, interrupting their problem-solving skills, their social skills, and their conversational skills. This plugged-in generation has some real consequences.

On one hand, we are trying to keep them connected to their friends, because this is how their generation relates to one another. On the other, we're trying to keep them connected to us—their parents—and to each other—their siblings—and in conversation with our voices that aren't in the realm of a text or a voice mail. Again, I don't think it's an all-or-nothing, feast-or-famine scenario. We don't say all and we don't say none.

I don't know if we're doing it right. I think they'll probably grow up and tell us all how we got this incredibly wrong. But we're doing what we think is the right thing. And sometimes that's all we can do.

One night when I was lamenting that I would rather be watching one of my shows than reading and journaling in silence, part of my brain interrupted this pity party with a string of questions: What are you really missing? Asinine television programming? Websites that suck you in, then waste your time? The Facebook knowledge that someone on my feed is on a tropical vacation?

These bits of information don't enrich my life in the slightest. They do, however, steal energy from my home and family, substituting face-to-face time with screens. We're all losing on this exchange, and it's my goal that we won't revert to the plugged-in family we were before.

The dangerous part of our social media and technologically saturated world is not its existence but what it distracts us from. We found quality time with family, focused our attention to conversation and creativity in planning our weeknights and weekends—all refreshing additions to our month. And while the Hatmaker clan resumed a very abridged schedule of TV and internet and gaming after our media-fasting experiment, we certainly gained a new perspective on them all.

I don't want to be addicted anymore, and I certainly don't want my kids to be slaves to these compulsions. So for now I'll continue to reduce and simplify, fight and engage until I know what else to do. What I know now is this: less. I don't need to have the most, be the best, or reach the top. It is okay to pursue a life marked by obscurity and simplicity. It doesn't matter what I own, what I watch, or how I'm perceived.

I'm just beginning to embrace the liberation that only exists where I have nothing to defend, nothing to protect. Where it doesn't matter if I'm right or esteemed or positioned well. I wonder if that's the freedom Jesus meant when He said, "Happy are people who are hopeless, because the kingdom of heaven is theirs" (Matthew 5:3). In order for Jesus's kingdom to come, my kingdom of noise and distraction will have to go, and for the first time, I think I'm okay with that.

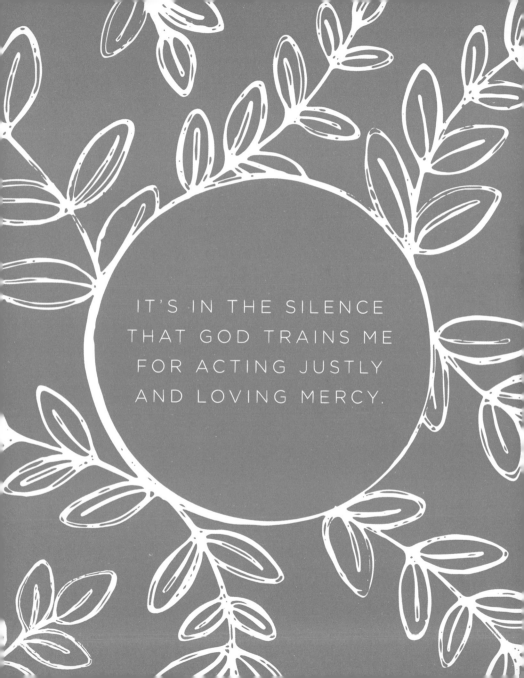

IT'S IN THE SILENCE
THAT GOD TRAINS ME
FOR ACTING JUSTLY
AND LOVING MERCY.

FIVE

TOSSING

*"The earth is the L*ORD*'s and everything in it,*
the world and and its inhabitants too.
Because God is the one who established it on the seas;
God set it firmly on the waters."

—PSALM 24:1-2

5

TOSSING

THE GREAT DISAPPEARING ACT

I don't know if you've ever gotten on a recycling kick, but if you have, you know that sometimes it can make you feel a little crazy. Seeing everything with new eyes, trying to be the best recycler the earth has ever seen, this new passion to protect our beautiful world can make a person act out of character now and then.

I know this because I drove by a neighbor's house on trash day recently. I do not know these people. But I saw a huge cardboard diaper box sticking out of their bin. So I stopped. I reversed. I pulled it out of their trash can, broke it down, and put it in our recycling bin instead because clearly, *they didn't deserve the box.* It might be the creepiest thing I have ever done. At least when it comes to someone else's trash.

The long and short of it is this—everything we eat, everything we wear, everything we purchase, it never actually *goes away.* Our food becomes the energy that fuels our bodies. When our clothes no longer fit us, we can donate them, recycle them in some way, or choose to throw them away in the trash. All of the packaging that accompanies our purchases can be recycled or tossed in the trash too. But just because it's out of sight and out of mind doesn't mean these things actually vanish. Except the food. Kind of. Actually, I would say that's more of a transformative process.

Anyway, I believe it's our responsibility to be responsible. And that means recycling when we can and composting if that's an option. Shopping with a conscience. Actually eating all the food we purchase or purchasing fewer items so we make sure we get through them all before our vegetables turn into stinky mush. It also means we need to acknowledge that when these items are no longer in our possession, they don't just disappear.

They end up in landfills or recycling centers. They require manpower and money to dispose of. In some cases, we're able to reuse these materials in the form of energy or recycled goods. But in other cases, that doesn't happen. Trash is buried or burned, which releases all sorts of things back into the ground, the water, and the air. *Cue the somber music and pan to a scene of a plastic water bottle floating down a river as an otter sheds a tear.*

No, this isn't an intro for a Sarah McLachlan commercial. What I'm saying is that I think it's important to understand the systems by which we move our waste and discarded goods so we can make smart and simple choices with our trash and the things we no longer need. That's it.

You may now return to your regularly scheduled program. And maybe bring a reusable water bottle next time you're out.

FAVORITES

Whether you live in a big city, the suburbs, or a rural town, there's no denying that all of these spaces look a million times happier and healthier (and support happier and healthier people) when there's an abundance of nature. Got a skyscraper? Add rooftop gardens. Have an apartment? Succulents are lovely and make any space brighter. Have a yard? Add some veggies and flowers. Got a farm or a large piece of land? Dig your hands into the dirt and walk barefoot on the grass as often as you can (while avoiding cow pies). I'm not so sure that the earth needs us to survive, but *we absolutely do need the earth*.

Part of Austin's charm is its green obsession, I mean, consciousness. Our law forbids residents or corporations from building on more than 20 percent of their land, to save the trees, vegetation, and wildlife. Austin is inhabited by recyclers, refurbishers, and repurposers.

And then there is me.

When we first moved to Austin, I spent far too much time worrying about how difficult it would be to start recycling. I swore I didn't have the time to be fussing with recycling bins and rainwater collection and remembering my reusable grocery bags and tree-hugging. I mean, it's just the earth. If we use it up and trash it into oblivion, it will regenerate, right?

So, so wrong.

Doesn't "creation" have something to do with God, whom I call "Creator"?

Surely God isn't worried about how we handle His creation that He created. His main concern is making His followers happy and prosperous, yes? And if we need to

consume the rest of His creation to make us happy, then I'm sure God doesn't mind.

In fact, I bet "creation" mainly refers to us humans, and the soil and rivers and animals and forests and oceans and wildflowers and air and vegetation and resources and lakes and mountains and streams are purely secondary, if not inconsequential.

That line of reasoning lasted for about five minutes in my mind until I realized how absurd it sounded. *Of course, we're supposed to take care of creation!*

It's like Wendell Berry wrote:

The ecological teaching of the Bible is simply inescapable: God made the world because He wanted it made. He thinks the world is good, and He loves it. It is His world; He has never relinquished title to it. And He has never revoked the conditions, bearing on His gift to us of the use of it, that obliges us to take excellent care of it. If God loves the world, then how might any person of faith be excused for not loving it or justified in destroying it?[18]

He might have a point.

Here are some suggestions for a greener and more simple life. Note that when it comes to most of these suggestions, the early steps may require more work or planning or money to acquire the necessary supplies. BUT, the long-term benefits far outweigh the initial investment.

- **COMPOST YOUR WASTE.** You can make (or purchase) a compost bin for your yard. There are also smaller composting bins you can purchase for your kitchen that will turn food scraps into dirt within days. Not possible with your setup? Ask a neighbor or a local garden if you can add to their compost waste. Pro tip: some community gardens allow the locals to come get dirt for their own gardens each year. And the cycle continues!

- **CONSERVE WATER.** The easy tip is to turn off the water when we aren't using it (even during long tooth-brushing escapades). What about taking a slightly less

boiling-lava-hot shower? (Cold water is good for the immune system and will wake you up in a hurry!)

- **RECYCLE (EVERYTHING, ALL OF IT).** Most cities have bins for both trash and recycling. You might have to take glass and batteries to separate locations, but if you make that a once-a-month trip, it's totally doable. Same for your cardboard if you don't want to cram it into your recycling bin. If you want to be both amazed and inspired, watch "Four Years of Trash: One Jar" on YouTube.[19]

- **DRIVE ONLY ONE CAR (FOR THE LOVE OF THE LAND) AND TAKE PUBLIC TRANSIT (OR BIKE OR WALK) WHEN POSSIBLE.** If you have more than one vehicle, try combining rides and errands. When it's nice outside (not snowing, sleeting, or raining frogs or locusts), this is a great opportunity to get some fresh air while getting a bit of exercise!

JEN'S TIPS AND TRICKS FOR LIVING LIGHTLY

Young parents: when they go to camp, save yourself the trouble of labeling everything, carefully packing toiletries and hygiene products, or the tomfoolery of sending each "daily outfit" in a gallon ziplock. They will wear the same socks all week and their toothbrushes will come home dry. This is a fact. Ask anyone.

- **BYOB.** Yep, that's right! Bring your own BAGS. This might be one of the easiest changes to make since multi-use bags have become more and more popular. Keep them in your car or by the front door so you remember to take them into stores with you.

- **BUT WHAT ABOUT PET MESS?** Now, I know, those of you who have pets use the grocery store plastic bags for pet poo, but there are better options.

Try BioBag Pet Waste Bags, PoopBags.com for biodegradable waste bags that actually biodegrade, and Flush Puppies Doodie Bags for flushable pet waste bags. *I am so excited I got to low-key talk about poop, I can't stand it.*

REFLECTIONS ON A SEASON OF SIMPLICITY

There have always been people who have cared about conservation and sustainability and global warming, but I think the scientists have finally convinced the rest of the world that the earth is actually in peril and is heating up. And unless we take pretty drastic global measures, the next few generations are in real trouble.

I see this as the great legacy of our generation, for good or for bad. Either we will be known as the generation who

took climate change seriously and made the monumental necessary reversals to protect the planet and future generations. Or we'll be the generation who continued to ignore every single alarm bell that has sounded to the detriment of our children and their children and their children. It will be daunting to see what happens next, and it's going to be upon us.

Ironically and unfortunately, we will experience the least amount of effects from our own choices. Our behaviors are going to have an outside effect on those countries that did not contribute to the world's climate issues to the degree that we have. Other changes are going to have to be located in policy and in legislation and in government. You and I have to begin reaching for reforms that are under our control and attainable while living normal lives.

If any one category in 7 had the most staying power with our family, it was when we learned to recycle, reuse, and conserve. A normal responsible consumer would have read that initial chapter and been like, golly, welcome to 1991. But we were so far behind that the huge pendulum swing for us was really profound and has stuck.

When my family made the decision to focus on recycling for an entire month, I was amazed at how many things we could actually recycle! We recycled glass, tin, cardboard, plastic, batteries, ink cartridges, paper, and cans. We upcycled glass spaghetti jars and filled them with detergent. Even our food scraps were recycled into compost and leftover water went to our sweet pup Lady's bowl.

I had bins for every category just inside the garage door. And where it was once common to have eight bags of waste crammed inside each trash can for the week, the first week we tried this, we put out one small trash bag for the whole week. ONE.

I admit for a period of time, recycling became an obsession. Remember my confession of recycling our neighbor's cardboard box? While I was extremely proud of what my family was able to accomplish in that month, I shuddered when I thought of how much we've tossed over the years that could've been repurposed.

The United States has 2,000 active landfills that are quickly running out of room.[20] The environmental issues these generate run the gamut from hazardous waste, toxic gas emissions, low-level radioactive waste to leakage into ground and surface water. When a landfill closes—because

no site can bury trash indefinitely—it must be monitored for thirty years because of the contamination threat. The health hazards posed cause much protestation and controversy, but there doesn't seem to be an easy answer.

Then there is the issue of volume, which even the most sophisticated system can handle for only so long. Americans generate trash at an astonishing rate per person, 258 million tons of municipal solid waste each year.[21] This is *twice as much* trash per person as most other developed countries. And if you think that's a lot (and it is), trash production has almost doubled since 1960, thanks to the onslaught of prepackaged everything-under-the-sun.[22] It's so convenient to us as consumers, but so detrimental to the environment.

This is an unprecedented problem as ours is the first society to generate disposable material by the millions of tons annually. Plastic bottles, containers and packaging, technology waste . . . these are the byproducts of "modern progress." And what do we have to show for it? Individually packaged cheese slices and deforestation.

Time to wake up and start making changes while we can.

FINAL THOUGHTS

"There is not always more. Except for our energy income
from the sun, the world is finite. Numbers of individual
organisms may seem limitless, but they are not. Species may
appear to be beyond counting, but they are finite in number.
Our life support systems may seem beyond abuse,
but there are limits to what they can bear.
Like it or not, we are finite creatures living in a finite world."[23]

—STEVEN BOUMA-PREDIGER,
FOR THE BEAUTY OF THE EARTH

In 2010, when I wrote 7, almost nothing was being delivered to our house. Amazon was just a fraction of what it was. All these home-delivery services weren't even in existence yet. And now literally anything can get delivered to your doorstep. Anything. I'm addicted to the convenience because time is my hottest commodity. Those services inject so many more hours back into my day since I'm not having to drive to a store, but I am considering their ecological impact.

After all, what does it mean to have to employ all these trucks and drivers and additional packaging? Right. It's a real bummer, and I wish I didn't care. But I'm taking this seriously; this knowledge is going to affect the way I consume delivery services. I believe I'll have to reform my actions around that shortly, and I'm dreading it.

Even twenty-five years ago, the popularity of bottled water was limited, but thanks to a clever industry who repackaged basic tap water and sold it to a society of convenience as a superior option, as if they collected it from the runoff of the Colorado Rockies, we now consume 100 billion gallons of bottled water per year, at a much greater price than drinking tap water.[24] Then into the trash, la-di-da. For the bargain price of a dollar, I receive sixteen ounces of tap water and contribute to the waste crisis.

Just when I was feeling tickled pink about my personal recycling efforts, I read this:

> *The most effective way to stop this trend is by preventing waste in the first place. . . . Waste is not just created when consumers throw items away. Throughout the life cycle of a product, from extraction of raw materials to transportation to processing and manufacturing facilities to manufacture and use, waste is generated. Reusing items or making them with less material decreases waste dramatically. Ultimately, less materials will need to be recycled or sent to landfills or waste combustion facilities.*[25]

By the time I put my glass in the recycling bin, it has already caused the lion's share of damage from processing and shipping. That knowledge gave me a jolt, but it also solidified my resolve to be a part of the change.

True reform involves purchasing fewer disposable materials in the first place, choosing bulk products, produce from the farmer's market, and secondhand goods that have already shed their packaging. Best practices include reusing containers over and over lowering the consumption of single-use materials. Recycling is probably a third-tier tactic toward genuinely reducing waste for maximum impact. So is it even worth doing? You bet your cotton bag of coffee beans it is.

A friend once said, "I don't know why you're trying. It won't matter. No one else cares." When she looked at the enormity of it all, she was discouraged. I, on the other hand, saw endless possibility and the great honor of doing what is right and good and true for our creation and our Creator:

If God is really at the center of things and God's good future is the most certain reality, then the truly realistic course of action is to buck the dominant consequentialist ethic of our age—which says that we should act only if our action will most likely bring about good consequences—and simply, because we are people who embody the virtue of hope, do the right thing . . . If we believe it is part of our task as earthkeepers to recycle, then we ought to recycle, whether or not it will change the world. Do the right thing. If we think it part and parcel of our ecological obedience to drive less and walk more, then that is what we ought to do. Do the right thing . . . We should fulfill our calling to be caretakers of the earth regardless of whether global warming is real or there are holes in the ozone layer or three nonhuman species become extinct each day. Our vocation is not contingent on results or the state of the planet. Our calling simply depends on our identity as God's response-able human image-bearers.[26]

Let's do the right thing. We really can make a difference.

I BELIEVE IT'S OUR RESPONSIBILITY TO BE RESPONSIBLE.

SIX

SPENDING

"Don't wear yourself out trying to get rich;

be smart enough to stop.

When your eyes fly to wealth

it is gone; it grows wings

like an eagle and flies heavenward."

—PROVERBS 23:4-5

6

SPENDING

Once upon a time, a woman was on a mission to understand where her money was going. She averaged how many different places per month her little family spent money. She tallied bank statements for the previous year, and they averaged sixty-six vendors a month, not counting repeat expenditures. She wanted to throw up. The end.

The next time you have a few hours and some extra counter or floor space, I challenge you to a duel! Er . . .

I challenge you to look through your bank accounts to see where your money goes. A week's worth—or two—of spending is a great start. You should be able to see some trends in a small space of time. But if you really want to get down and dirty, review the last three to six months, or better yet—a full year's worth of spending—to get a fuller picture.

You might want to have a barf bag nearby.

Or maybe not. Maybe you are the queen of budgeting and you know exactly where you spend your money, right down to the very last cent. In that case, please share your gift with all who will listen! Because this is a big deal, and we need your wisdom.

Families fall apart because of money issues. Countries go to war because of it. Our livelihoods and communities depend on it. And since there are over 2,300 Bible verses about money, you'd think we'd be better about our spending and saving, right?

Uh, no.

Allow me to blow your mind: the average American has about $38,000 in personal debt, excluding home mortgages, and 25 percent of this is credit card debt.[27] Heck! I have a confession about credit card debt a little later, but for now, just know that if this represents your current reality—there is an LED light at the end of the tunnel.

You know, I think it was easier to keep track of what we spent and where back when people used checkbooks. Remember them? You'd have to write a check and make a note in the register for the date, where you purchased an item, how much it was, and then—THEN!—you had to deduct that amount from your total. That's

right. We had to do math on the spot in order to keep up with our spending habits.

Not anymore. With online banking, credit cards, Venmo, PayPal, and the like, it's far too easy to disassociate with money. We see something we want, we click a button and it arrives on our doorstep in a few hours or a few days. That's far too easy! And convenient, let's be honest.

But many of us are spending it faster than we make it and feel like we're always playing catch up. Stop the madness!

I want to encourage you to take control over your money again. That might mean you need to take a long, hard look at your potentially nonessential purchases (Starbucks, eyelash extensions, subscription fees, fast food five times each week) and see where you can cut back a little or a lot. Maybe altogether in some cases.

If you're feeling personally attacked by any of the aforementioned items, it's okay. I know some people become maniacal without their coffee, so for Pete's sake, keep on keeping on. But see if you can make adjustments elsewhere in your spending habits and, also important here, set a goal. Do you want to see if you can save an extra $20 a week? What about paying off a car loan or a credit card a few months early? What about saving for a house? Or raising money to adopt a sweet angel child who is meant to be part of your forever family?

Whatever your financial goals, I guarantee there's a creative and simple way to reach them without turning your whole life inside out. The first step is to be aware of where the money goes in the first place.

FAVORITES

When Brandon and I got married in college, many years ago, our joint income was $11,270. In a whole year. We were poor through the early days of youth ministry and into the lean days of one income, babies, and toddlers.

I remember Brandon once handing me a twenty-dollar bill to feed our little family for a week. The refrigerator and pantry were empty, I had a preschooler at the table, a toddler on my leg, and a baby on my hip. I sat in the middle of our kitchen and bawled my eyes out.

Maybe you've been there too.

Food insecurity is a terrible feeling all around. Add children into the mix and your anxiety goes through the roof.

Back then we didn't just watch each penny; we scrutinized, counted, shuffled, and squeezed every last one. Going to Sonic for a hamburger and a drink was an outrageous extravagance. Buying new clothes? Not going to happen when the babies needed diapers and food. We were surviving and trying to make the best of it. And lured by the temptation of more, we made the decision to live outside our tiny means.

Staying true to our generation, over the years we dug a deep, dark debt hole to purchase the lifestyle we couldn't afford but, for some reason, felt entitled to. We lived paycheck to paycheck, floating checks and nodding politely as the wealthy people at church talked about their vacations and new cars, wondering who we had to make out with to acquire these luxuries. (Credit card companies were all too happy to oblige.)

It was a terrible cycle and caused many arguments and sleepless nights. And it took many years to extricate ourselves from the cycle of debt and food insecurity. Was it hard work? You'd better believe it was. But absolutely worth it.

I'm thankful I no longer fill my gas tank half full or feed my tribe of seven on twenty dollars a week. And I'm well aware that for many families in our community, and across the globe, they're making do with much less.

We've conquered that debt and—brace yourself—we even have a savings account. Once I finally quit panicking that my debit card would be declined every time I used it (which took years in the black to overcome), the pendulum swung to the other side. Still a mess, but a mess with some disposable money. *Heck.*

When I sat down and realized how and where and when we (read: I) spent our money, I felt that familiar wave of anxiety kick in. I had been completely careless. And clueless. Anyone who spends money in sixty-six places a month is the most heinous kind of consumer.

How will I answer for my choices when God confronts them one day? With this much expendable income funding restaurants, shoe stores, and movie theaters, I'm certainly doing my part to keep our economy rolling along, but what am I doing to help my family's economy? Or to provide for those in my community? I doubt Jesus will accept my excuses for neglecting the poor on account of cash flow.

So! Here are some tips Brandon and I used to get a handle on spending.

- **WRITE DOWN YOUR FINANCIAL GOALS.** It can be easier to forego a few regular (but maybe not necessary) purchases for a period of time if we have a goal in mind. Saving for a house? Paying off a credit card? Need to update your computer? Write it down, including how much you'll need to save to accomplish the task.

- **MAKE A BUDGET AND STICK TO IT.** Seems simple, but you actually have to do it. You don't need any fancy accounting software. But you will need a few hours and a way to track and add up all of your expenses. Some like Excel spreadsheets. Some like pen and paper. No matter which method you choose to tally up your expenditures, it will be enlightening for sure!

- **CUT THE FAT.** This is where you'll need to have some serious talks with yourself. Instead of eating out three times a week, what if you cut back to one? Are you actually using all of your music and media subscriptions, or can you pause one or two for a while?

Have a membership to the gym that you haven't used in over a year? I know a gal who kept up her YMCA membership for three years without going once, just in case she decided to use it one day. Hundreds of dollars down the drain! I'm not advocating for unhealthy habits, but if you aren't using a gym membership, maybe it's time to save your money and find another way to exercise that inspires you.

• **GET CREATIVE.** Can you take on a part-time or seasonal job for a few months? Can you child-sit or mentor others in your community for an hourly rate? Can you sell any items you have that are sitting around collecting dust? Can you start a YouTube channel where you bake cookies and dance to '80s rock music? I mean, have you seen some of the ways people are making money these days? Expand your mind and expand your wallet.

REFLECTIONS ON
A SEASON OF SIMPLICITY

As a family of seven, we spend a lot of money. Combing through a year of bank statements, I found clarity and resolve. It turns out that we are not big-ticket item buyers, but we do nickel and dime ourselves to death. We spend almost everything we make, and honestly, I can barely account for half of it.

This was why spending had flown under my radar most years. The majority of the purchases were subtle, incremental, and seemingly inconsequential. Just this little thing here and that small thing there. I don't feel like cooking; let's just get this. Individually, nothing too egregious, but together, our spending amounts to a startling number.

Big deal, right? Do I really need this high-end lipstick when I could easily find a drugstore brand in the same color? Does it actually hurt someone if I buy these name-brand jeans or does it help someone if I don't?

Let's say I cut my spending down and work toward less consumption, using what we actually have and finding joy in the simplicity of less. If I took the time and effort to change my ways, would my choices even matter? Would yours?

I think they might.

If you want an idea of just how backwards our spending trends really are, just look at these numbers I pulled while I was doing research on the first 7-experiment:

Annual US spending on cosmetics: ....**$8 billion**
Basic education for all global children: .....**$6 billion**

Annual US and European
spending on perfume:...............................**$12 billion**
Clean water for all global citizens: ....**$9 billion**

Annual US and European
spending on pet food: ....**$17 billion**
Reproductive health for all women: ....**$12 billion**[28]

Shocked yet? Consider these figures about social and economic injustice:

Socially and economically, we have created great disparities of wealth. A minority of the world's population (17%) consume most of the world's resources (80%), leaving almost 5 billion people to live on the remaining 20%. As a result, billions of people are living without the very basic necessities of life—food, water, housing and sanitation.[29]

And if these percentages from 1998 seem too muddy to grasp, these numbers from a 2014 study will make it all too clear: "Nearly 1/2 of the world's population—more than 3 billion people—live on less than $2.50 a day. More than 1.3 billion live in extreme poverty—less than $1.25 a day."[30]

We are the minorities, living high on the hog, buying the majority of the stuff while half the world's population

can't even afford a fast-food value meal each day. And we've been living like this for decades.

We are the 20 percent at the top, buying more than 80 percent of the stuff.

When we imagine the enormity of it all, it might very well feel like we can't possibly make a difference. And, in truth, maybe *one person* changing their spending habits wouldn't matter.

But if hundreds and thousands then millions of us challenged the paradigm—and we said no for every two times we said yes and acknowledged the power of our consumer dollar—then our generation could turn the ship around. And you know what that tidal wave of change starts with?

One person.

You.

Me.

Making a difference and showing others that it is not only possible but imperative.

It takes true courage to change. Could we be countercultural enough to say, "We're not buying that. We don't need that. We'll make do with what we have. We'll use the stuff we already own."

If this causes anxiety, I'm with you, trust me. Because who curbs their appetites anymore? Who uses old stuff when they could buy new stuff? Who sews patches on jeans or uses last year's backpacks? Who says no when they can afford to say yes?

We could.

FINAL THOUGHTS

"But your loyal love, Lord, extends to the skies;

your faithfulness reaches the clouds.

Your righteousness is like the strongest mountains;

your justice is like the deepest sea.

Lord, you save both humans and animals.

Your faithful love is priceless, God!

Humanity finds refuge in the shadow of your wings.

They feast on the bounty of your house;

you let them drink from your river of pure joy.

Within you is the spring of life.

In your light, we see light."

—PSALM 36:5–9

In the original experiment, one of the hardest months was deciding the seven locations for the month where we were going to spend money. Again, that was back before I was spending a great deal of money online.

So now with a million online options, spending is just ubiquitous. And it's typically not big spending. It's little amounts here and there.

I think there are some really interesting and creative ways to reduce spending. The clothes swap, of course, is one of my favorites and is also fun. Buying thrift is a great way to redirect our spending dollars to a different pool. And there's an idea of sharing.

I live in a smaller community in a suburb of Austin, and all my closest friends and several of my family members live right here. So we share a lot of big-ticket items or items that we don't use a lot, but when you need them, you need them. Those include lawn mowers, leaf blowers,

pressure washers, monogram machines. We have a whole entire party-in-a box kit that has candles and lanterns and stuff to decorate with when you're having a little dinner party or whatever. And we share all that.

Rather than everybody purchasing one, we have some items that are up for grabs all the time. Whether it's among a friend group or a group of neighbors, one way to continue to decrease spending is to share the goods!

I heard this line of reasoning recently and it stuck: "Just because I can have it doesn't mean I should." Yes! It hit me so hard I nearly high-fived the stranger next to me.

When we think about this logically, it totally makes sense, right? But it's also unfamiliar since we often hear excuses advocating for the opposite point of view around spending:

- It's no big deal.

- I can afford this.

- I deserve this.

- I've worked hard for my money, so I can spend it how I want.

- I want this, back off.

- Other people spend *way more.* (Guilty. This is my excuse of choice.)

- I still have money in the bank so it's fine.

- What's the big deal?

I wish I had back so many indulgent and seemingly insignificant purchases. The irresponsible and selfish and vain spending I've endorsed is so staggering, I hope never to know the actual number lest I sink under it.

BUT.

We can move forward. We can change the way we spend and save and think about money and where it goes.

One way to change is to be okay with nonconsumption. Use what we have over and over instead of always seeking the new.

Two, we can redirect all that money saved toward paying off our debt, toward padding our savings and retirement accounts, and toward helping our community and the causes we hold dear.

Three, it's time we become wiser consumers.

We can simply stop spending so much, use what we have, borrow what we need, repurpose possessions instead of replacing them, and—the kicker—live with less.

In the face of the world's suffering and the inequalities created by corruption and greed, we actually hold immense power for change, because we decide where our dollars go. If enough of us decided to shift our perspective and take action, we would unleash a torrent of justice to sweep away disparity, extreme poverty, and hopelessness.

The world is waiting. Our kids are watching. Time and resources are wasting. Are we willing?

I know I am.

IT TAKES
COURAGE TO
CHANGE.

SEVEN

STRESSING

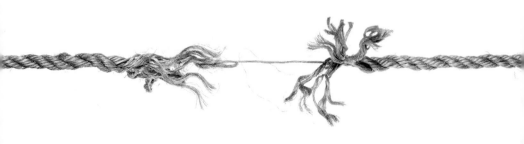

"Only in God do I find rest;
my salvation comes from him."

—PSALM 62:1

7

STRESSING

BURNING AT BOTH ENDS

What causes you the most stress?

What doesn't cause me stress, you're chuckling.

Work. Family. Bills. Traffic. News. What you're going to eat today. What you're not going to eat today. That meeting that will last an hour longer than it should. Screaming kids. Shedding pets. Lack of sleep. Lack of caffeine. Too much caffeine. A too-full calendar. Not having enough time to relax for just a few minutes and think. *Can I get an Amen and a nap?*

Girl!

I get it.

Sometimes it's hard for a season. And sometimes it's hard for what seems like years. Somehow, we keep going. The world turns. We make it through. We become wiser. And hopefully, we discover what is really important and what is not.

When I inspected my calendar, I counted five blank squares in eight weeks. Five. Only five nights in two months where I didn't have something planned, somewhere to be, something to do, some event that requested my participation.

Sound familiar?

We have too much going on. We are short-fused, stressed out, overextended, and unrested. This pace is not sustainable without the real possibility of breakdowns and burnouts and stress-related illness. Not surprisingly, there are multiple ways that stress affects women differently and more frequently than men, including: tension headaches and migraines, depression and anxiety, heart problems, upset stomach, obesity, problems becoming pregnant and problems with our menstrual cycle, and a decreased sex drive.[31] Listen, I don't know about you, but this dang list of issues stressed me out by just reading it.

I don't want it to be this way. No, thank you. This season of life is passing me by, accelerated by a lack of boundaries, of feeling as though I should say yes to everything when I should say no to a lot of things, when I could—and should—be advocating for my own space, my own sanity, and a simple, joyful existence.

Most days I just try to keep the wheels on, getting it done while thinking about what's left. But you know what that leads to? My kids and husband get half-answers, and we all feel the tension. If I don't make the time for myself and my family, I can guarantee you that life is not going to magically make time for me.

This is the ridiculous American life. Every one of my friends has a similar story. None of us are happy about it,

yet we keep filling the calendars. *Yes, I'm in; we'll sign up; I'll do it.* We race from one activity to another, teaching our children to max out and stress out. Nice legacy, right?

All the while, the biblical concept of rest is whispering to me, "You're ignoring me." And I am. How can I rest, recharge, and tune in to what and Who matters most if I'm so preoccupied with *doing* that I don't make time for simply *being*?

Busted.

I feel like I'm burning at both ends.

Luckily, since I'm the one who makes my schedule, I can break the crazy cycle and learn to prioritize my God, myself, and my family above all the busy.

It also helps that I have a secret trick to combat stress.

It's true! I have employed it more times than I can ever count. And it works on every single human in the family! It works 100 percent of the time on 100 percent of the people.

Our kids have an increased amount of stress as their lives get more complicated and more mature and more sophisticated, so they will frequently bottle up all their anxiety, keep the lid on it at school all day, but come home and just entirely fall apart. You know, that is what home is for. It's supposed to be a safe place. But that means we are the recipient of the lion's share of their anxiety.

Years ago when my kids were coming home absolutely boiling over and irrational, I thought, *You know what? A bath works for me. Maybe I'll just try it with them.* So I started the tradition of the "awesome bath." I don't care if it was four o'clock in the afternoon, if they came home snippy, I'd say, "How about I draw you an awesome bath?" And I mean *awesome*. I used oils and bubbles and delicious sea salts. I set up a little table by the bath and I lit a candle for them. I'd bring in a speaker and play their favorite music and make them a cute little snack on a plate and pour something to drink in a pretty glass and set it on the table.

And I am telling you, this works *every single time*. Water is soothing. And I will tell you this works on boys. This is not just a girl strategy. It even works on husbands!

Sometimes when all the frustrated-mad-sad words are out, there's nothing else to say. If you cannot convince that person you love to calm down or that it's going to be okay, create an awesome bath for them (or something equally indulgent and wonderful if you don't have a bathtub). I am telling you, 45 minutes later you will witness a miracle as they emerge a new person.

And it works on you too.

FAVORITES

Do you ever pray for peace, for guidance, or for support? Have you ever wondered what happens in the spiritual realm when we pray? It's such a mystery. Does God wait for us to pray in His will, primed to move for righteousness? How many relationships is He waiting to mend? How much turmoil is He poised to soothe? How much peace is He ready to administer? And would it help speed up the process if I did a specific dance and prayed specific words in order?

I do know that He urges us to forgive, release, lay down, let go, trust, offer, submit, rest, and obey; these are the keys that turn the locks that bind. Like Jesus promised: "I'll give you the keys of the kingdom of heaven. Anything you fasten on earth will be fastened in heaven. Anything you loosen on earth will be loosened in heaven" (Matthew 16:19).

God is inviting us into this spiritual relationship in every moment, with every breath. He's advocating for our happiness, for our best days, for us to enjoy our work and be with our families and friends, instead of letting the world run us ragged every second of the day.

You know what we need to do? Make the time.

Whether you decide to revise a week, a month, or the rest of your beautiful life, know that ultimately you are in control of your time. Not your job. Not your kids. Not your favorite TV series. You get to say yes or no to every request, and I'm hoping you decide to make yourself a priority and let everything else fall into place, or fall off the calendar entirely.

Here are some ideas to help prompt a calendar and life overhaul:

- SCHEDULE REST AND RELAXATION DAYS IN ADVANCE. No, it's not being selfish. It's called self-care and it will help keep you sane during stressful times. We have such an aversion to making time for ourselves that it's the first thing that gets bumped when our calendar is overloaded. But wait! You can't give your best to your family, your job, your hobbies, or your community if you are running around frazzled and half-crazy all the time because you refuse to care for your own needs. Need a massage? Book it. Need a nap? Take it. Need a weekend getaway with no email access? Make it happen.

- **PRIORITIZE QUIET TIME IN THE MORNING AND AT NIGHT.** You don't have to set aside a full hour to pray. Sometimes even a few minutes of silence and gratefulness is all you need to set the tone for the day. Same thing at night. Before bed, take a few moments to be thankful for all you accomplished. *Didn't accomplish squat?* You survived the day anyway! Be thankful for that, and for the opportunity to do it all over again tomorrow.

- **LET OTHER PEOPLE KEEP THEIR CRAZY.** As women, moms, sisters, friends, coworkers, aunts, and grown-up daughters, we have a natural tendency to be fixers and doers and helpers and listeners. Nothing wrong with that. Until we take on other people's drama as our own. Eek! Don't we each have enough to worry about without also having to second-hand stress about fifteen other people's woes? Hear me out—I'm not saying we shouldn't genuinely care about others or help them when in need. What I am saying is that we should be aware when we discover we are carrying around baggage that was never ours to begin with. It's called boundaries—emotional, physical, electronic, or otherwise.

Ask for help. Look, you don't have to go it alone. Life is beautiful but it's also downright cruel sometimes. If you need help of any kind, reach out to your friends and family, to your local resources, or to a licensed professional. It's incredibly courageous and cathartic to talk through questions, doubts, pains, and sadness alongside someone who truly wants you to succeed. While stress can cause a lot of negative space in our lives, it's also an opportunity to be seen and heard and to know we're not alone in a chaotic world. You have incredible worth, many talents, and a big life ahead of you. Reach out, chin up, heart open. You've got this, sister!

JEN'S TIPS AND TRICKS
FOR LIVING LIGHTLY

Isn't it so true that between the laundry and carpool and baseball practice and workload and volunteering and endless projects and family management and just ALL THE HUSTLE, it is so easy to forget the most basic, beautiful truth?

That God loves us so much.

Like, He is over the moon for us, just like any parent who is lovesick over the kids.

REFLECTIONS ON A SEASON OF SIMPLICITY

One of my greatest joys is spending time at my parents' ranch. Now, I realize when I say *ranch* you might be imagining a luxurious, rustic mansion with overstuffed leather furniture and antler chandeliers. But no, dear reader. That is simply not true.

This is a working cattle ranch, no house, just a barn that houses a four-hundred-square foot office/living room/kitchenette/bathroom, including a utility sink, refrigerator, and washer and dryer. During the winter we fight over who has to hand wash the dishes while bundled like an Eskimo. The pipes freeze at the first sign of a cool breeze, so we keep milk jugs of water in the bathroom so we can fill the tank up and flush.

At night the two couches fold out into beds—voilà, a bedroom. These beds are slightly less comfortable than sleeping on an inverted mat of ball bearings. We have no internet and no cell phone service. There is no cable either, but we do have one spotty TV with a VHS player where we watch old movies every night, piled on the couches like puppies. We'll wear the same clothes over

and over, and four days into our stay, I'll ask if anyone has taken a shower. The answer will be no.

The ranch life is a simple one, depleted of all the extravagances we're addicted to.

And yet, once a visit has been scheduled, none of us can wait to get out there. We love the ranch and every rustic detail. We crave the outdoor air and dirty farm boots. The kids explore for hours on the four-wheeler. We would have no clue where they were if not for the hilarious walkie-talkie communiqué we eavesdrop on.

With twelve deer blinds on the ranch, Brandon and the boys experience pure bliss from their hunting endeavors. As the sun sets and the hunters are returning, I start dinner and enter that grateful transition from the activity of the day to the relaxation of the evening.

I love gathering my chicks after days like that, when muscles and imaginations have been stretched to their limits and flushed cheeks walk in the door, competing for space to tell their tales. Hats are pulled off and ponytails released, a mountain of ranch boots left by the door. The family assembles with fresh, new memories and an eager anticipation of the next day.

This is the connection I long for. The simple gifts of conversation, time, good food, and no reason to rush. I want more—no, I need more—of this in my life. And I imagine you need more in your life too.

More of less.

More peace.

More beautiful silence.

More laughter.

More joy.

Good news! It's right here, waiting for you.

FINAL THOUGHTS

"Dear Artist of the Universe, Beloved Sculptor, Singer, and Author of my life, born of your image I have made a home in the open fields of your heart. The magnetic tug of your invitation to grow is slowly transforming me into a gift for the world. Mentor me into healthy ways of living. Help me remember to pause."[32]

—MACRINA WIEDERKEHR,
SEVEN SACRED PAUSES

The rhythm of the ranch is healing to the frantic pace of normal life. It's also a tutor, teaching me the superior tempo of living well. At the ranch there is no hurry. There is no racing from one thing to the next unless you count trying to outpace sweet Lady Bird on the four-wheeler.

Perhaps the greatest gift of a break like this and a place like this is clarity. When almost everything else besides my family is inaccessible, I realize that my mission becomes concentrated: this matters, this doesn't, this counts, this doesn't.

It's actually not that complicated.

I know not everyone has a place where they can physically retreat to recharge. But can you close a door and find silence for an hour? Can you open a window and turn off all of your devices and dream? Can you walk outside barefoot, sit at the dinner table with your family (and without phones and a TV), and share all the many reasons why you love them?

Can you love yourself? Forgive yourself? Make friends with yourself? Speak kind, encouraging words to yourself when you don't feel your best?

Friends, change begins with us and ripples through our homes, into our communities and our world. One smile at a time. One kind word at a time. One healthier decision at a time.

It *is* healing to forgive.

You *do* gain your life by losing it.

Love *does* truly conquer evil.

A simple life really *is* liberating.

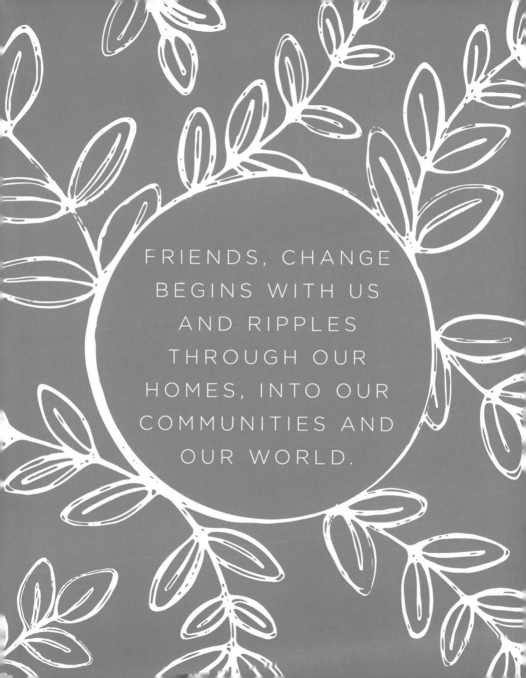

FRIENDS, CHANGE BEGINS WITH US AND RIPPLES THROUGH OUR HOMES, INTO OUR COMMUNITIES AND OUR WORLD.

FINAL
THOUGHTS

"The Lord bless you and protect you. The Lord make his face shine on you and be gracious to you. The Lord lift up his face to you and grant you peace."

—NUMBERS 6:24-26

FINAL THOUGHTS

ABOUT SIMPLICITY AND LIVING LIGHTLY ON THE EARTH

Once in a publishing meeting, I was asked, "Who is your reader?" and that got me thinking about you. I'm going to guess you are probably a middle- to upper-middle-class parent (but love to my nonbreeders!), and mostly your life is terribly blessed. Your world is pretty controlled: kids are in good schools, neighborhood is safe, jobs are fairly secure, wardrobe is impressive enough. These advantages cause you some tension, but you're not sure why or what to do with it.

You're likely a believer, but whether you're a lifer or a recent devotee, I'm not sure. A few of you are teetering on the edge of faith, drawn in by Jesus but repelled by his followers.

As for church, you might go to one, but a bunch of you don't—the elitism and waste and bureaucracy became too much and you left or you want to leave or you vowed to never return.

Some of you are solid attenders, but you feel like crawling out of your skin sometimes, valuing faith community but worried yours is missing the point. A few of you have found the church of your dreams. Half of you read *Radical* or *Crazy Love* or *The Irresistible Revolution*, and since you're reading this, you might have read *Interrupted*. You loved and hated it.

I'm guessing you've cried over orphans or refugees or starvation or child prostitutes, heartbroken by the depravity of this world. It's not okay that your kids get school and birthday parties while children get abandoned and trafficked, but you don't know how to fix that. You're wondering if your lifestyle is connected to these discrepancies, and you have a nagging suspicion that less is more, and that a simple life might yield less stress, but it's a muddy concept.

Truth is, everyone has ideas. It's confusing and overwhelming. This creates a sort of war within, and it leaves you raw. Sometimes you're a full-blown mess over it.

Hear this: I don't think God wants you at war with yourself.

He sent the Prince of Peace to soothe those tumultuous waters already. Self-deprecation is a cruel response to Jesus, who died and made us righteous.

Guilt is not Jesus's medium. He is battling for global redemption right now; His objective hardly includes huddling in the corner with us, rehashing our shame again. He finished that discussion on the cross. Plus, there's no time for that.

We're so conditioned to being a problem that we've forgotten *we're actually the answer.* God is not angry at you; how could He possibly be? You are His daughter; you're on the team. Don't imagine He is sitting us all down for a lecture. Rather, He's staging a rally, gathering the troops.

If your stuff and spending and waste and stress are causing you tension like mine is, just do the next right thing. Ask some new questions; conversation partners are everywhere. Take a little baby step. Tomorrow, you can take another. And offer yourself the same grace Jesus has given you. We're no good to Him stuck in paralysis.

As I've continued on this journey of simplicity, I've discovered I can fast from clothes and waste and spending easier than I can fast from busyness.

Wear the same outfit six days straight? Sure.

Garden and recycle? No problem.

Rework my daily schedule so I have time to pray, time to read, time for silence, time to focus on my work, all the while saying no to things I don't really want or need to do? Now that's asking a lot.

I've found this work to be very challenging and equally beautiful. The quest for a simpler life taught me something: my heart craves a slower life.

I want to figure out what that would look like for our family. I know we can't live in my parents' barn forever, nor can we pull out of work, ministry, school, community, mission, family, and all the activities that accompany them. But what can we do to cultivate a quiet ranch heart in a noisy urban world?

We all need a break. Perpetuating a busy life doesn't just affect me, but my entire household, my extended community. The pace we keep has jeopardized our health and happiness, our worship and rhythms. We belong to a culture that can't catch its breath; rather, we refuse to catch our breath.

But little by little, I can sense that even our small changes are beginning to make a big difference. When we live with intention and love like today is all we have, those small ripples eventually make big waves.

Keep these truths in mind as you step into this new season of simplicity. They will serve you well so that you can serve everyone you meet—including yourself—with grace and understanding:

- Love God most. Love your neighbor as yourself. This is everything.

- If we love God, then we will care about the poor.

- This earth is God's and everything in it. We should live like we believe this.

- What we treasure reveals what we love.

- Money and stuff have the power to ruin us.

- Act justly, love mercy, walk humbly with God. This is what is required.

As I wrap up *7 Days of Simplicity*, I'll quote a prayer written by Henri Nouwen which resonates so deeply, it's as if he stole my thoughts:

> *Dear Lord, you have sent me in to this world to preach your word. So often the problems of the world seem so complex and intricate that your word strikes me as embarrassingly simple . . .*

> *Let me retain innocence and simplicity in the midst of this complex world. . . . Do not allow evil powers to seduce me with the complexities of the world's problems, but give me the strength to think clearly, speak freely, and act boldly in your service.*[33]

MY FAVORITE SOURCES

A FEW COMPANIES WITH A CONSCIENCE

www.livefashionable.com
www.furnacehillscoffee.com
www.preemptivelove.org
www.noondaycollection.com
www.globalgirlfriend.com
www.3seams.com
www.ravenandlily.com
www.numanainc.com
www.nisolo.com
https://legacycollective.org
www.camanoislandcoffee.com
www.consciousstep.com
www.thegivingkeys.com
www.thistlefarms.org
www.tenthousandvillages.com
www.joynbags.com
www.renewproject.org
www.mytradesofhope.com
www.truthbecomesher.com
www.ssekodesigns.com

NOTES

Introduction

1   "The Problem with Plastics," Ocean Conservancy, https://oceanconservancy.org/trash-free-seas/plastics-in-the-ocean/.

2   Emily Holden, "US Produces Far More Waste and Recycles Far Less of It than Other Developed Countries," July 3, 2019, *The Guardian*, https://www.theguardian.com/us-news/2019/jul/02/us-plastic-waste-recycling.

3   Derek Thompson, "2.6 Trillion Pounds of Garbage: Where Does the World's Trash Go?" June 7, 2012, *The Atlantic*,https://www.theatlantic.com/business/archive/2012/06/26-trillion-pounds-of-garbage-where-does-the-worlds-trash-go/258234/.

4   Holden, "US Produces Far More Waste."

Chapter 1

5   Taylor Wolfram, "Sustainable Eating," February 15, 2019, Academy of Nutrition and Dietetics, https://www.eatright.org/health/lifestyle/culture-and-traditions/sustainable-eating.

6   Michael Pollan, *In Defense of Food: An Eater's Manifesto* (New York: Penguin, 2008), 10.

7   See http://www.eurekalert.org/pub_releases/2005-03/chb-eoc031605.php.

8   Barbara Kingsolver, *Animal Vegetable Miracle: A Year of Food Life* (New York: Harper Perennial, 2007), 126–27.

Chapter 2

9 Jane Wheeler, "Clothing of the 1830s," ConnerPrairie.org, https://www.connerprairie.org/educate/indiana-history/clothing-in-the1800s/.

10 Tera Harmon, "Closets Through the Ages: The History of Closets in Residential Homes," February 1, 2018, Get Organized Columbus, https://www.getorganizedcolumbus.com/closets-through-the-ages.

11 Morgan McFall-Johnsen, "The fashion industry emits more carbon than international flights and maritime shipping combined. Here are the biggest ways it impacts the planet," October 21, 2019, BusinessInsider.com, https://www.businessinsider.com/fast-fashion-environmental-impact-pollution-emissions-waste-water-2019-10.

12 Benjamin R. Barber, *Consumed: How Markets Corrupt Children, Infantilize Adults, and Swallow Citizens Whole* (New York: WW Norton, 2007), 9–11.

Chapter 3

13 "Calculate Your Carbon Footprint," The Nature Conservancy, https://www .nature.org/en-us/get-involved/how-to-help/carbon-footprint -calculator/.

14 Richard Rohr, *Simplicity* (New York: Crossroad Publishing Company, 2003), 59–60.

Chapter 4

15   Matt Richtel, "Attached to Technology and Paying a Price," June 6, 2010, *New York Times*, http://www.nytimes.com/2010/06/07 /technology/07brain.html

16   Ashley Rodriguez, "Americans Are Now Spending 11 Hours Each Day Consuming Media," July 31, 2018, Quartz, https://qz.com/1344501 /americans-now-spend-11-hours-with-media-in-an-average-day-study/.

17   Abigail Hess, "Here's How Many Hours American Workers Spend on Email Each Day," September 22, 2019, CNBC.com, https:// www.cnbc.com/2019/09/22/heres-how-many-hours-american-workers -spend-on-email-each-day.html.

Chapter 5

18   Wendell Berry, *What Are People For?* (New York: North Point, 1990), 98.

19   Lauren Singer, "Four Years of Trash: One Jar. What's in Lauren Singer's Mason Jar?" YouTube, January 4, 2017, https://www.youtube .com/watch?v=OuABgFsv5pw.

20   Joe McCarthy, "Where Will The Trash Go When All the US Landfills Are Full?" May 14, 2018. https://www.globalcitizen.org/en/content /us-landfills-are-filling-up/.

21   McCarthy, "Where Will The Trash Go".

22 "National Overview: Facts and Figures on Materials, Wastes and Recycling," Environmental Protection Agency. March 13, 2020 https://www.epa.gov/facts-and-figures-about-materials-waste-and -recycling/national-overview-facts-and-figures-materials.

23 Steven Bouma-Prediger, *For the Beauty of the Earth: A Christian Vision for Creation Care* (Grand Rapids: Baker Academic, 2010), 20.

24 Magnus Jern, " How many people consume bottled water globally?" October 29, 2018. https://tappwater.co/us/how-many-people -consume-bottled-water-globally/

25 "Reduce, Reuse, Recycle," https://www.epa.gov/recycle.

26 Bouma-Prediger, *For the Beauty of the Earth*, 182.

Chapter 6

27 Megan Leonhardt, "Here's how much debt Americans have at every age," August 20, 2018, CNBC.com, https://www.cnbc.com /2018/08/20/how-much-debt-americans-have-at-every-age.html.

28 "The State of Human Development," United Nations Human Development Report 1998, chapter 1, 37.

29 World Centric, "Social & Economic Injustice," http://www .worldcentric.org/conscious-living/social-and-economic-injustice.

30   DoSomething.org, "11 FACTS ABOUT GLOBAL POVERTY,"
     https://www.dosomething.org/us/facts/11-facts-about-global
     -poverty#fn1; Original data from: United Nations Development
     Programme. "Sustaining Human Progress: Reducing Vulnerabilities
     and Building Resilience." Human Development Report, 2014.

Chapter 7

31   "Stress and Your Health," https://www.womenshealth.gov
     /mental-health/good-mental-health/stress-and-your-health.

32   Macrina Wiederkehr, *Seven Sacred Pauses* (Notre Dame, IN: Sorin
     Books, 2008), 177.

Final Thoughts

33   Henri Nouwen, *Seeds of Hope* (New York: Doubleday, 1997), 112.

ACKNOWLEDGMENTS

The most heartfelt thanks to my little family, the recipients of all my "ideas." Ten years after the original 7 experiment, we are still practicing tons of what we learned. How wonderful. To Brandon, Gavin, Sydney, Caleb, Ben, and Remy, you are the family of my dreams. Thank you for not moving out when I confiscated all your screens for a month.

Yet again, I'd like to thank the original Council for 7: Jenny, Shonna, Trina, Molly, Becky, and Susana. You helped see through the project in every way, and now it has a new iteration which you deserve credit for. Your support kept the ship afloat. I don't know why any of you ever say yes to me, but I sure love you for it.

I feel so tender toward the team at Abingdon Press for this new version of 7 focusing on a simple, sustainable life. You have been an utter joy. Thank you for your creativity;

you brought real life to this project. I am a delighted new member of your publishing community. You were the perfect home for 7 *Days of Simplicity*.

So much sincere love to Austin New Church, the safest, kindest, bravest little faith community I ever did know. I have learned alongside of you what it means to surrender. You've taught me to love my neighbor in wild, shocking ways. I trust you. I am your grateful sister.

ABOUT THE AUTHOR

Jen Hatmaker, sought-after speaker, Big Sister Emeritus, and Chief BFF, is the beloved author of twelve Bible studies and books, including *New York Times* best sellers *For the Love* and *Of Mess and Moxie*. Jen hosts the award-winning *For the Love* podcast and leads a tightly knit online community where she reaches millions of people each week in addition to speaking at events all around the country. Jen and her hubby, Brandon, are founders of Legacy Collective, a giving community that grants millions of dollars around the world. The couple lives on the outskirts of Austin, Texas, with their 5 kids—Gavin, Sydney, Caleb, Ben, and Remy—in a 1910-era farmhouse that they overhauled as the stars of the HGTV series *My Big Family Renovation. Fierce, Free, and Full of Fire* and *7 Days of Simplicity* are Jen's latest books.